Raw Power!

Building Strength And Muscle Naturally

Stephen Arlin

Published by
Maul Brothers Publishing
San Diego, California

Raw Power!
By Stephen Arlin

Disclaimer:
This book is not intended as medical advice because Mr. Arlin does not recommend the use of cooked foods or medicines to alleviate health challenges. Because there is always some risk involved, the author, publisher, and/or distributors of this book are not responsible for any adverse consequences or detoxification effects resulting from the use of any procedures or dietary suggestions described hereafter.

First Edition: August 1, 1998
Cover Art: Ken Seaney, Ground Zero Graphic Design
Special Thanks To: David Wolfe

ISBN #0-9653533-1-1

Printed in North America by
Maul Brothers Publishing
PO Box 900202
San Diego, CA 92190 USA
(619) 645-7282

Acknowledgment

This book is dedicated to the truth and health seekers of the world. Perfect health is our natural birthright and there is one way to attain and maintain perfect health -- by total adherence to, and living in harmony with, the Laws of Nature. All human problems can be traced back to a fundamental breaking of those laws, beginning with the cooking of food. It is my intention to provide you, the reader, with new insights into these laws that are always there for us to use at our disposal if we are just brave enough, and intelligent enough, to trust in them. The person who can completely trust in, and live by, these laws is the true genius, a genius bred for self-mastery.

Also By Stephen Arlin:

Nature's First Law: The Raw-Food Diet

How To Win An Argument With A
Cooked-Food Eater

IS Philosophy

Raw Power! (video)

Table Of Contents

A Word From The Author

Just over 4 years ago, I remember thinking, "If The Raw-Food Diet cures so-called 'incurable' illnesses and rejuvenates old, tired, and diseased bodies, what would happen if someone who was relatively healthy with no health problems at all adopted The Raw-Food Diet?" Well, that thought led me and my organization to the greatest discovery in the history of the world -- Paradise Health. Our organization in San Diego, California U.S.A. is called "Nature's First Law." We have written a controversial raw-foods book entitled **Nature's First Law: The Raw-Food Diet** and we are out there every day releasing a little bit more of this vital message to the world.

It was the reading and self-education we did on health, diseases, and diet that led us to The Raw-Food Diet. We focused only on success -- success stories, people who had healed themselves of disease, people who lived the longest and healthiest, people who had traveled and observed human beings all over the world. We did not focus on the standard medical dogma, because that has all been a failure. There is more disease, sickness, and misery now than ever before in human history. We started bouncing some ideas off of each other and we really got into some amazing things.

It was tough at first because cooked food is addictive and getting over any addiction is tough -- but worth it! For every disciplined effort in life there is a multiple reward. Once I cleansed my body of the cooked-food residues, I no longer craved cooked food. What a liberating experience! I can sincerely tell you -- it is magical. When I went all-raw, I opened up the natural part of my consciousness that was being kept locked up in a dark dungeon all my life. I see the world much more clearly now. Every day is a great day. All my desires become realized instantly now. It may sound strange, but it is the truth.

As soon as I realized that eating cooked food was unnatural and that it was the cause of all human health problems, I took massive raw-foods action. I just did my best each day to go without cooked food and I didn't worry about how much raw plant food I was eating. There is a saying: "Every amount of raw plant food is better than any amount of cooked food." I used to eat a lot of raw food back then, but that subsided as soon as I got over my cooked-food addiction. I stopped eating cooked food completely after about a year. I eat only raw plant foods because it is our natural diet -- and nothing unnatural can sustain itself for very long.

The level of health I have attained is indescribable, incomprehensible, and unfathomable to people who haven't experienced 100% raw-foodism. It's the difference between night and day. It's the difference between an inner-city slum and a tropical paradise. I shed 51 unwanted, unhealthy pounds (238 to 187 -- I'm 6'2") and have since then gained back 25 pounds of healthy, solid muscle through the unique training work-outs and 100% raw-plant-food diet outlined in this book.

I currently eat (by weight) about 70% raw, organic fruit, 25% raw, organic, green-leafy vegetables, and 5% raw, organic nuts and sunflower seeds. Note that I'm using the botanical definition of a fruit which is: A fruit is something that contains the seeds within itself for regeneration of the plant. (Avocado, tomato, cucumber, squash, pepper, etc. are all botanical fruits.)

This diet is easy, once you know the facts. No one could have the discipline to do this diet if there wasn't something going on biologically. Eating cooked food has nothing to do with the normal biological requirements of the cells. Any food put to flame becomes addictive. Once you break away from that you open yourself up to the most incredible discovery of all time. This message is really the most powerful personal development strategy put forth by anyone.

Today's heresy is tomorrow's orthodoxy. We represent a force of resistance against enormous odds. We are at the forefront of a movement which proposes to reshape the world. Therefore, we serve the future and not just the passing hour. The greatest and most enduring successes in history are those which were least understood in the beginning, because they were in strong contrast to public opinion and the majority views and wishes of the time. Every great idea once began on the fringe.

There is a lot of conflicting information in the world today, especially in the field of nutrition. However, there is one thing that is certain: every living organism on Planet Earth is designed to nourish themselves with raw nutrition, humans are certainly no exception. A raw-foodist is not something you become, it is something that you already are. Every single natural organism on the planet eats exclusively raw foods. No free-living creature ever tampers with its food. Some people consider this diet the next step past a vegetarian or vegan diet, but it really transcends all diets. It is simply the natural way to nourish your body. The Information Age, in many ways, has become overbearing and obsolete. Listening to and acting upon your own body's natural instincts, desires, and needs is the way to Paradise Health, not by listening to someone else's dietary dogma.

Stephen Arlin
August 1, 1998

Chapter 1

Introduction to Raw Power!

This book is about attaining a level of health that is our absolute birthright -- Paradise Health. It is about: eating a 100% *natural* diet, *true* natural body-building, and *total* fitness. What is known to the world as "Natural Body-Building" is hardly natural at all. Just because someone trains steroid-free, doesn't mean that they are building a natural body. Food is the foundation of everything that we are physically. If you are eating unnatural food, you are engaged in "Unnatural Body-Building." The only way to truly build your body is through eating naturally. This book does not waste much time presenting arguments in favor of The Raw-Food Diet. It assumes that the reader already has a basic knowledge of what true natural nutrition is -- raw food. If you do in fact want a comprehensive overview of the entire philosophy of natural raw-food nutrition, I recommend first reading **Nature's First Law: The Raw-Food Diet** by Arlin, Dini, and Wolfe.

Every living organism on planet Earth is a 100% raw-food eater; not 99%, not 70%, not 50% -- 100%! There are trillions of organisms and creatures on this planet that are thriving and living virtually disease-free eating 100% raw foods. There is only one organism that tampers with its food -- the human organism. *Trillions to one!* Those are staggering odds. That would make the likelihood that we should be eating cooked food about 100,000 times more improbable than winning the lottery. You don't want to bet against those kind of odds. Eat all raw!

I know raw-foodists all over the world, in just about every country. I have met raw-foodists that live in inner cities; I have met raw-foodists that live in tropical paradises. The point is, no matter where you live, no matter what condition you live in, you can make the change and eat 100% raw foods -- every living organism on this planet does it, and so can you.

Most health-seekers give up on The Raw-Food Diet when their weight drops and the peer criticism and self-doubt begins. This book is designed to help you reach the next level, to surpass the negativity, and to build a body filled with super-strength and energy!

When you begin the process of undertaking The Raw-Food Diet you will lose weight. It is inevitable. After years of eating cooked and processed dead foods, your body becomes loaded with toxic material. For example, the only way to clean a bathtub filled with dirty water is to first pull out the plug and completely drain. Once the body has a chance to unload poisons, it will do so. Each organ will cleanse itself, every tissue will purge dead material. The body will

detoxify. This is always accompanied by weight loss -
- "the good will push out the bad."

This detoxification process is the major barrier
to achieving a 100% raw-food diet -- especially if you
are a bit advanced in years. Cooked food clogs up your
body and stops detoxification. Cooked food is never
beneficial. Cooked food is an abomination. So to
properly detoxify, you must combat cooked-food
addiction. Get the cooked food out, bring the raw food
in! How do you clean-up the river, as long as the chemical plant is dumping waste?

Do you remember the concept of diffusion from
chemistry class?   Molecules move from areas of
greater concentration to areas of lesser concentration.
As the blood thins out on The Raw-Food Diet, toxic,
undigested molecules trapped in the lymph will pour
into the blood.

As one keeps rinsing, washing, and polishing
the membranous tract, one may experience recurring
symptoms of past illnesses. Coughs, colds, headaches,
mucus eliminations, diarrhea, sore throats, fevers,
rashes, pains that float from one part of the body to
another, and the negative mental states of anxiety,
depression, and imbalance, may reappear as one per-
sists with a natural lifestyle of raw foods, exercise, and
sunshine. Your weight will fall.

To win through, you must endure all these dis-
comforts, even if you have to relive (for short periods
of time) old sicknesses experienced as far back as your
teens. The toxins and wastes responsible for old sicknesses, which may have lain dormant since infancy,
will be released from their hiding places. You may
even taste a medicine you ingested years back, or have
a craving for a food you have not eaten in decades. I
have tasted breakfast cereals not eaten in fifteen years
which have suddenly hit my tastebuds.

The cycles of purge and replenishment may last
weeks, months, or even a couple years. It all depends
on your lifestyle before. It depends on how toxic your
body is. Everybody goes through a different detoxification process. *Embrace the detoxification process,
accept it, and get past it.*

During the detoxification period and the initial
stages of raw eating you can, and should, exercise the
muscles and strengthen the body. While exercising,
you may experience light-headedness and other detoxification symptoms. You may not feel as strong,
because your body is using all of its energy to cleanse
and rebuild itself. Always do what you can, where you
are, with what you have. Start walking and build up
from there if that's what it takes.

You will not put on healthy weight until the
body is sufficiently cleansed. Again, this may take a

couple of months for some people or a couple of years for others, depending on their age and the toxic conditions of their bodies. In my case, I lost 51 pounds (23 kg) initially. I dropped from 238 pounds (107 kg) to 187 pounds (84 kg) and stayed at that weight for 4-5 months when I was transitioning. Then I quickly gained 15 pounds back (6.8 kg) (by exercising and eating exactly the same raw food) and have steadily been gaining weight ever since, until now I weigh approximately 212 pounds (94.5 kg) -- I'm 6'2" tall.

Everybody can gain all the strength and healthy weight they want, in any parts of their bodies they choose. Whether you want to gain 10, 20, or 30 pounds (4.5, 9, 13.5 kg), you can! If you gain just one wholesome pound per month, in one year, you will gain 12 pounds (5.5 kg)! Remember, your bodyweight is 50% muscle.

Look at every part of your body in the mirror, daily, in the nude. Look for challenging areas. Exercise where you need development. The areas of your body you consider to be thin or underweight are the areas upon which you should focus your attention and energy.

On The Raw-Food Diet, it is easy to gain muscle and unleash a hidden strength and potential if you will persist past the negativity and peer pressure. No great success is possible without persistence. Change your peer group if necessary. Get away from toxic people. Water seeks its own level, and you can rest assured that people will try to bring you down to their level.

It's definitely not an overnight transformation, although you can start to see results immediately. You obviously can't expect to be in perfect physical shape by working-out once. And the same is true with any-thing for that matter. Fundamentals practiced daily and consistently produce massive results.

To gain healthy, muscular weight, you must do all you can of the following:

1. think powerfully!
2. completely eliminate cooked food, drugs, medicines, and animal foods from your diet
3. intense, progressive, resistance exercises
4. sunbathe & airbathe nude
5. maintain your emotional poise
6. be free of toxins
7. fast whenever ill
8. sleep
9. meditate
10. avoid overindulgence in sex

The four major, important factors that go into gaining strength and healthy, natural weight are: Mind, Diet, Exercise, and Sunlight.

Chapter 2

Power Of The Mind

Human potential is unlimited. There is no point where your memory is too strong, your creativity too high, your thought process too clear, your intuition too strong, or your extra sensory too powerful -- there is no ceiling! The human mind is truly amazing.

The most important factor in attaining the exact physique that you desire is mind, or attitude. Have you heard of "The Self-Fulfilling Prophecy"? If you truly believe something, it is more likely to come true. If you truly make a concerted effort to gain muscle and healthy weight, you can do it. You must conclusively decide that you *want* to gain strength and weight and make it your number one priority. Write down your goal weight and physique on paper (in your journal). To achieve your goal, a vision of the peak is needed, for the first step depends on the last. Imagine or picture your body as it will look like when you achieve your goal physique.

When the going gets tough, it is always the mind that fails first, not the body. What you think about, comes about. Monitor, closely, the conversation and pictures which you allow to fill your mind.

Affirm in your own mind, "I am strong; I am powerful; I am unstoppable; I can gain strength and healthy weight each day." Look at yourself in the mirror and emotionally tell yourself "You cannot be stopped; You are energized; You are unlimited." This is the mindset of a winner. Do you think Olympic athletes beat themselves up daily with their own thoughts? No way! Winners first become winners in their minds. They affirm their own capabilities daily, either in their conscious mind, out loud, on paper, or all three. You must do the same. As long as you are thinking "I am weak," you will be weak. Weak thoughts lead one to progressively identify with weakness. Challenge yourself, use your mind to strengthen your determination, strength, and resolve. Do it, never doubt it. One doubt, and you're out.

The idea that incredible strength and healthy weight cannot be built on a raw-food, vegetarian regime is simply that... an idea. An idea that has absolutely no basis in fact. The 200-pound (91-kg) body of the orangutan, the 500-pound (227-kg) body of the gorilla, and the 3,000-pound (1,364-kg) body of the elephant are all constructed of 100% raw plant food. I am here to settle your mind and demonstrate to you that great size and strength can be accomplished naturally by humans too.

You have the potential to create the exact body you want. You can restructure and rejuvenate your body by rethinking yourself, by grasping on to a wider vision of yourself. De-program your old thought habits and re-program yourself for mind mastery. Send down a different body plan to your subconscious mind through affirmations and pictures of your ideal self. With consistency, your body and experience will follow suit.

Anchor and maintain a powerful belief system. The most important pre-requisite for accomplishing any goal and for becoming a vibrant, powerful raw-foodist is a powerful, undiminished belief that what you are doing is indeed the only normal and natural way to live. This belief must be the product of your own conclusions. This underlying belief must be strong enough to carry you through the cyclical lows in the process of attaining your goal. Chance, destiny, and fate cannot circumvent, hinder, or control the firm resolve of the determined. We know nothing until intuition agrees. Half-measures never have and never will achieve the desired results.

As you engage in vigorous exercise, leverage your mind by focusing or meditating on your strength and physique goals. Do not allow yourself to be dis-tracted. Listen to high-energy music while training (I listen to progressive heavy metal music when I train!). Some people think that heavy metal music is negative and depressing, but it's not. Progressive heavy metal music is powerful. Some high-energy bands I highly recommend listening to while training are: Fates Warning, Nevermore, Symphony X, Iced Earth, Queensryche, and Dream Theater.

Chapter 3

The Raw-Food Diet

The most important element of health is diet. Of course, food isn't everything, but it is the foundation upon which everything else is built. Everything that you physically are right now was once the food that went into your mouth, the air you breathed, the water you drank, etc. Other important factors in health are: positive thoughts & associations, sunshine on the skin, empowering relationships, exercise in Nature, interaction with animals, clean air, unpolluted water, and avoidance of mass media.

What we eat deeply and radically affects how we think, feel, and behave. In fact, it directly affects how we interact with our planet. Switching to a raw-food diet has a *massive* positive impact on the environment as well as ourselves. The principle I am describing here is very simple. Life change comes from the inside out. Once you change on the inside, everything changes on the outside.

The most valuable aspect of raw-foodism is its transformative value. You're not the same person just a little bit healthier on The Raw-Food Diet. You become a *radically* new person with new interests,

goals, and aspirations.   As co-author of my book
Nature's First Law: The Raw-Food Diet David
Wolfe says, "We are not really human beings, we are
human becomings, because we are constantly becoming something more." How profoundly true!

A major problem that most people have is: eating for emotional reasons. Never eat until you are
hungry. Every cell and part of your body must be exer-
cised before you eat so that the food you eat will be
properly metabolized. Create a demand for the food
every time you eat. Earn your food. If you put the best
food in your body when you are not hungry to eat, the
food will not be assimilated at the most efficient level
and it will drain energy unnecessarily.

Here are some good guidelines to keep in mind:

1. Do not eat when fatigued
2. Do not eat immediately before beginning
   exercise
3. Do not eat when in pain
4. Do not eat when under mental or physical
   distress
5. Do not eat when ill
6. Do not eat when there is a severe inflammation
   of some area of the body
7. Do not eat cooked foods
8. Do not eat non-vegetarian foods
9. Do not overeat

10. Do not eat foods containing pesticides
11. Do not eat additives, chemicals and/or other synthetic products

Throw out any and all bread. You cannot build strength on bread. Eating bread makes you as flimsy and as pliable as the bread itself. Bread also contains an enormous amount of estrogen (a female hormone). If you are male, it has the propensity to throw your sexually way out of whack. I've seen it happen many times! Stack the odds in your favor by not eating it.

Immediately throw out all medication and supplements (pills, powders, liquids, etc.) of any kind. Medications and supplements are poisons and the body must go through a tremendous internal crisis to eliminate and detoxify them. A "poison" is anything taken into the body that cannot be metabolized and utilized effectively by the body, and that the body must waste resources on eliminating and/or detoxifying (greater than any benefit received therefrom). Processed substances and supplements are never beneficial. They have been massively denatured. Pills and powders are not natural, of course. All the information and pseudo-science fed to the masses about the supposed "benefits" of these denatured supplements is erroneous, hypothetical, and inspired by greed. To say that a pill or powder is beneficial is saying that Nature has made an error by not offering us these foods in a processed, refined state -- which, of course, is ridiculous. The Raw-Food Diet and periodic fasting is the best way to cleanse the body of toxicity, not pills and powders!

The mythology spun together by colloidal representatives may sound good, but an astute and logical mind knows otherwise. Many colloidal minerals sold for consumption come from clay or dirt. Humans are not dirt-eaters. A colloid is a mineral suspended in solution with energy. Colloids are the fundamental building units of our physical body and should be eaten in their living state within raw fruits and vegetables.

Remember, you have to detoxify *all* the toxic waste and poisons out of your body, and keep them out, before you can build up on raw foods. You have to be willing to detoxify *all* the way. Again, you can't clean up the river as long as the chemical plant is dumping waste upstream! Our bloodstreams are our most important rivers. It is easily possible to gain muscle and unleash strength that you never knew you had if you simply adhere to the Laws of Nature.

What people must understand and accept is the fact that for every disciplined effort in life, there are multiple rewards. I've seen people go through very mild detoxifications, and I've seen some pretty hard-core detoxifications. It really depends on how you lived your life before. Someone who was a heavy drug user, medicine taker, or smoker is obviously going to have a heavier detoxification than someone who lived their life more in accordance with the Laws of Nature. The Laws of Nature are there for you to use to your benefit. Human progress through knowledge has been solely and exclusively a chiselling away at the distinctions which define the Laws of Nature. The greatest insights in history have been by those who revealed a new distinction about Nature (which was actually there all along). When the body gets buried in unprocessed residues of cooked foods and finally has the energy to release them, it will. *There is no magic pill, only a magic process.* As we untangle ourselves out of the cooked-food residues, we release suppressed toxins and emotions. Hang in there, understand what is happening. Read materials on The Raw-Food Diet, stay active, get outdoors, and enjoy the abundance life has to offer! Don't worry about detoxification symptoms, they are clear signals that your body is healing.

Fasting is the fastest way to heal the body. A good guideline is to fast one day a week. The problem with raw food is that it actually contains too much nutrition! Giving your body a rest one day (or more) a week is great. Newcomers to The Raw-Food Diet need not worry about fasting until they have been 100% raw for at least 6 months. It is best to educate yourself first on the subjects of raw-food diet and fasting and take one step at a time, initially just stopping the intake of cooked food and progressing from there.

Steroids are an abomination. Cooked-eating, meat-eating, pill-popping, steroid-injecting body-builders have false, cooked, artificial strength. They have truly accepted a Faustian bargain (A short-term gain at the expense of a long-term tragedy). Sooner or later, they will have to pay the price. And they do, as we see among most of the retired body-builders and athletes whose bodies have fallen apart by the time they reach the age of fifty.

Eat the foods you like; eat foods which agree with you. Since everyone is a bit different, everyone should eat a bit differently, according to their natural instincts, desires, and environments. Eat only foods which you feel satisfy your nutritive needs, digestibility, and assimilation. What is desirable for you, may not be desirable for someone else.

No cooked food is benign. Cooked food acts malignantly by exhausting your bodily energies, inhibiting your healing process, and decreasing your alertness, efficiency, and productivity.

Eating cooked carbohydrates, dead proteins, and burned fats, leads to an internal accumulation of numerous mutagenic (carcinogenic) products caused by the cooking process.

When you treat food with thermal fire, you destroy the life-force in food. The heat of cooking destroys vitamins, enzymes, nucleic acids, chlorophyll, de-animates minerals, and damages fats, turning them into dangerous trans-fatty acids. These changed fats are incorporated into the cell wall and interfere with the respiration of the cell, causing an increase in cancer and heart disease. The heat disorganizes the protein structure, leading to a deficiency of the amino acids. The fibrous or woody element of food (cellulose) is changed completely from its natural condition by cooking. When this fibrous element is cooked, it loses its broom-like quality to sweep the alimentary canal clean. The fibrous matter is changed from its natural state to a poison. As I say over and over in my book **Nature's First Law: The Raw-Food Diet**, -- "Cooked food is poison." Fire destroys, it doesn't create anything. When you add flame to something, it becomes less than it was before. If you don't believe me, try adding flame to your house. Will it become more or less than it was before? Well, the same situation exists with your food. If you add heat or flame to it, it will become less than it was before. The ramifications of cooking are massive.

Eating cooked food suppresses the immune system. After eating cooked foods, the blood immediately shows an enormous increase of leukocytes or white blood cells/corpuscles. The white blood cells are supposedly a first line of defense and are, collectively, popularly called "the immune system." This spontaneous multiplication of white corpuscles always takes place in normal blood immediately after the introduction of any virulent infection or poison into the body since the white corpuscles are the fighting organisms of the blood. There is no multiplication of white corpuscles when raw plant food is eaten. The constant daily fight against the toxic effects of cooked food unnecessarily exhausts the body's strength and vitality, thus causing disease and the modern shortness of life.

Ingesting cooked food allows inorganic minerals to enter the blood, circulate through the system, settle in the arteries and veins, and deaden the nerves. After cooking, the body loses its flexibility, arteries lose their pliability, nerves lose their power of conveying expressions, the spinal cord becomes hardened, and the tissues throughout the body contract. In many cases, this dead matter is deposited in the various joints of the body, causing enlargement of the joints. In other cases, it accumulates as concretions in one or more of the internal organs, finally accumulating around the heart valves. A lack of flexibility in any area of life, especially in the physical body, causes premature aging and weakness. The importance of stretching the body and returning the tissues to a natural elasticity cannot be overstated.

Raw foods are easily digested, requiring only 24-36 hours for transit time through the digestive tract, as compared to 40-100+ hours for cooked foods.

Prolonged digestion creates putrefaction and disease in the colon. It robs energy which could be directed towards gaining strength. Remember, digestion takes more energy -- by far --than any other internal bodily activity.

On The Raw-Food Diet you will experience the elimination of body odor and halitosis (bad breath). Eating raw will also alleviate allergies because cooked foods irritate the delicate, thin mucus lining in the body and sinuses. Eating raw allows space for free-breathing and a better internal environment for vigorous physical training.

Dr. Karl Eimer experimented with top athletes in Germany, producing improvement in their performance by putting them on a 100% raw-food diet. Raw plant food provides you with more strength, stamina, and energy because it has the best balance of water, nutrients, and fiber which meet your body's needs precisely.

On The Raw-Food Diet, the mind (memory and power of concentration) will be clearer. You will be more alert, think sharper and more logically. So, raw foods not only allow you to build a real base of healthy strong muscle tissue, but they also allow you to focus more clearly, especially when exercising.

Raw foods will not leave you with a tired feeling after a meal. There is a tendency towards lethargy after a cooked meal. When eating raw foods you require less total sleep and you will experience a more restful sleep. This allows more time to achieve goals and enjoy exercise activities with friends and family.

Raw foods are delectable, delightful, and delicious and have more flavor than cooked foods. Cooked food is dead and bland. That is why people need to doctor-up cooked food with ridiculous additives. These "flavor-enhancing" (stimulating) additives irritate your digestive system and overstimulate other organs. Avoid the following harmful additives: refined sugar, table salt, black pepper, bottled spices, and all other condiments.

Nature clearly demonstrates, in the eating habits of every form of life, the basic principles of nutrition. Animals, in their feeding, obtain a balanced intake of basic food components so that the ratio of sugars, fats, proteins, carbohydrates, mineral salts, and vitamins to each other remains basically the same.

The plant is the basis of all animal life on Earth; all animals deriving their food either directly or indirectly from plants. Eat raw, fresh, organic fruits and vegetables to supply the requisite vitamins and minerals. Eating these will minimize digestive stress and conserve bodily energy. A minimum of digestive power should be expended in order to obtain a maximum of nutritional return. Again, eat only those foods which you can most readily digest and assimilate.

Humans belong to a species class called a frugivore, or fruitarian -- i.e. a fruit eater. Practically all frugivores include green vegetables in their diet. Chlorophyll-rich foods are the blood of life. The chlorophyllous green, leafy vegetables are the richest sources of alkaline mineral salts, living carbohydrates, and top-quality proteins. The most complex laboratory in the world resides in the photosynthetic green-leaf organs of plants. The leaves contain an excess of organic base compounds in a colloidal form.

Eating animals and animal products is not only unnecessary and not within our biological design (see Appendix B of **Nature's First Law: The Raw-Food Diet**), but is extremely harmful to your health. All heart disease has been directly linked to the unnatural consumption of animal products and a wide variety of other diseases and ailments also find their basis in the consumption of animal products. But, can you gain strength and muscle without eating meat? Just ask vegetarian Bill Pearl, who won 4 Mr. Universe bodybuilding titles. Arnold Schwarzenegger once said, "Bill Pearl never talked me into becoming a vegetarian, but he did convince me that a vegetarian could become a champion body-builder."

There are also massive mental repercussions

from eating animal products. The link between vio-
lence and eating animal products is a well-known fact.
Can you imagine that the primary way in which people on this planet interact with animals is by eating
them? INSANE!

My partner in health, David Wolfe, has noted in
his book **The Sunfood Diet Success System** that all
long-term raw-foodists he has met and/or interviewed
eat out of the following classes of foods:

1. Green-Leafy Vegetables (wild greens being
   the best)
2. High-Water-Content Sugar Fruits (melons,
   tropical/subtropical fruits, etc.)
3. Fats (avocados, coconuts, nuts, seeds, dried
   olives, durians, etc.)

These three food classes form the essentials of
The Raw-Food Diet. These foods balance against each
other and keep you centered. Think of the three food
classes as corners of a triangle, the center being the
balance point. For example, when one eats too many
fatty foods, the internal propensity (or instinct) is to eat
more greens and juicy sugar fruits to balance. Or, if
one eats too many juicy sugar fruits, the internal
propensity (or instinct) is to eat more greens and fats
to balance. Or, if one eats too many greens, the internal propensity (or instinct) is to eat more fats and juicy
sugar fruits to balance. Keep this in mind as you

develop a consistent raw-diet which can catapult you to your maximum potential.

For maximum strength and body-building, eat a large green-leafy salad each day. Organic or home-grown romaine lettuce or black kale are probably the most superior leafy-vegetables nutritionally and they are the most palatable when eaten alone. Use also the chlorophyll-rich and mineral-saturated wild greens such as dandelion, malva (mallow), lamb's quarters, thistle, etc. -- the more natural your food, the better. Also, celery (the favorite food of the gorilla) is a fine addition to the body-builder's diet. Celery provides organic sodium which balances out the potassium of fruits providing a balanced internal chemistry. Cut up an apple or an avocado and mix it with your salad if you find it dry.

Eat the salad slowly. Fletcherize your food. Dr. Fletcher taught that each mouthful of food should be chewed at least 50 times before swallowing. An ancient Indian proverb states: "Chew your food well, for the stomach has no teeth." Thoroughly mix the salad with your saliva. The more your food is ground up and chewed, the greater will be the absorption by the body. Lack of intestinal absorption is a major rea-son why people have trouble gaining weight. Typically, the cooked-food eater's intestinal tract is lined with a mucus layer which prevents nutriments from passing through the intestinal villi. This mucus must be broken up and dissolved to restore the proper functioning of the intestinal tract. I recommend a series of colon irrigations to jump-start the cleansing process. Also, there are certain foods which efficiently dissolve mucus, such as the fig. The fig is ranked as one of the highest mucus dissolvers in Ragnar Berg's Table in Arnold Ehret's book **Mucusless Diet Healing System**.

Of course, raw-plant foods improve the total inner environment. Raw food greatly enhances the efficiency of nutrient absorption. Over time, The Raw-Food Diet enables the body to dislodge accumulated wastes from the intestinal folds and to remove accumulated intestinal mucus.

The foods which are best for human consumption are the fruits. They are our most natural food. Fruit is where it is at. Try to eat non-hybridized fruit (fruit with viable seeds) and wild fruit. I do not buy into the "hypoglycemia is caused by fruit" idea, even if it is hybridized commercial fruit. I do believe, from experience, that a good percentage of the fruits you eat should be non-sweet fruits such as cucumber, red bell pepper, tomato, corn, and zucchini. I also believe that fruit causes a cleansing of refined sugars out of the body which may have been stored there for years -- even decades. Never, for your sake, ever eat refined sugar of any kind (that includes the sugar found in bread and other cooked starches).

To adopt a frugivorous diet, find one or more staple fruits which you like so much, they make you feel as if you can live off of them alone. I personally prefer melons, berries, avocados, and citrus fruits.

You most certainly can build muscle on a frugivorous diet, especially if you engage in rigorous anaerobic exercise. This is how to build muscle mass. It is funny that people believe you can build muscle out of cooked animal muscle, but not on fruits and green-leafed vegetables! Cooked animal muscle is a dead, lifeless, coagulated substance; raw fruits and vegetables are perfectly designed and contain everything your body requires in a simple, usable form.

Though it is not totally necessary, for ideal digestion, eat one type of fruit at a time. Try not to mix different types of fruits together. Follow a "mono-diet" when eating fruit. Eat foods that are in season (see Appendix D). Eat the heavy fuel or "high-calorie" fruits such as apples, avocados, bananas, cherimoyas, dates, durians, grapefruits, lemons, limes (ripe, not green), mangos, etc.

Nuts are also a potent food, especially in the winter season. I do not like to use the word "moderation," but remember to moderate with nuts. You can get "nutted out." Eat nuts with naturally-dried apricots or raisins for superior digestion (My experience has shown that eating dried apricots or raisins and nuts in

the Winter increases one's resistance to cold weather).
Nuts are a heavy food which can provide you with
heavy fuel or calories for long, intense workouts.

Protein is a heavy building material which
appears abundantly in nuts (relative to other plant
foods), but is also available in vegetables and even
fruits. Cooked protein is coagulated and dead.
Cooked proteins simply clog the tissue system causing
the muscle tissue to puff up. Strength is gained at the
expense of vitality and the body is put under a tremendous strain to prevent damage to the ligaments and
joints. Adequate, raw proteins help you to gain desirable weight, but are not necessary in large amounts.

The gorilla is the strongest land mammal pound-
for-pound. A gorilla has the strength equivalent to
bench pressing 4,000 pounds (1800 kg)! Gorillas eat
primarily green-leafy materials, which are the real
body builders. Of course, the gorilla is a 100% raw
plant eater! Do you think if a gorilla ate bread, meat,
cheese, candy, etc. every day it would be able to perform feats of strength like this? I think not.

Raw proteins are built out of simpler substances
called amino acids. Of the 22 necessary amino acids,
there are eight which our bodies must get from outside
sources. All of these eight are present in raw plant
foods -- especially in green foods -- in their correct
proportions. Think of a cow which is 1,000+ pounds

(450 kg) of protein flesh. What does a cow eat? Grass. All the amino acids necessary for the cow to build an enormous body are present in grass, and any green plant for that matter.

To gain strength and healthy weight, I also recommend sending "hot" food through the intestinal tract on a regular basis. Pick your favorite "hot" raw foods, whether they be: garlic, onions, ripe hot peppers, ginger, etc. You can juice these foods with vegetables, mix them with salads, or eat them in a monomeal. "Hot" foods burn out parasites and stimulate the intestines. I have noted, particularly with children turning on to raw-food, that excessive thinness is associated with parasite infections. Now, I know that Natural Hygienists believe these foods to be irritants... and they are irritants... to parasites in your body! I've been to Natural Hygiene conventions and let me tell you, most of the people there look like something out of "Night of the Living Dead." A good axiom to follow is: "Don't listen to anyone, in any field of information, if they are not receiving the results that you desire." You wouldn't go to a beggar on the street for financial advice would you? Well, don't take the advice of out-of-shape, emaciated, sickly, unhealthy people!

Dead food, negative emotions, and inactivity drain your energy and cause weight loss. This becomes definitely more true the closer you get to a

100% raw diet. My experience has shown that one cannot reach her/his ideal body weight unless the body is significantly purified by a 100% raw-diet. Those who linger close to 100%, but do not actually achieve it will not be able to perfectly gain the weight they desire. One may even gain up to 10 pounds (4.5 kg) by moving from 98% raw food to 100% raw food!

Remember, cooked food (even a small amount) drains and dehydrates your body of precious, heavy, living water. Living water is derived most abundantly from living plants, especially fruit. Living water is not just filtered water which comes through the roots and into the plant; living water is actually created during photosynthesis. Living water is heavier, more electri-fied, and has greater solubility properties than ordinary water (the hydrogen atoms are pulled together more tightly in each molecule of living water, thus giving the molecule greater polarity).

Living water weighs more on a molecular level than dead tap or spring water (the 60 trillion cells mul-tiplied by the slightly heavier water-weight of every molecule produces a big difference in overall body weight). So you will gain weight on raw food as long as you are 100% raw. I could not gain weight until I went 100% raw. The water stored in my body would go towards diluting and digesting bread and dead food and I would feel drained. Whenever I would eat any-thing cooked I would become sallow and lose 5 to 10

pounds (2.3 to 4.5 kg)! Commit yourself -- go 100%
raw. It is *not* extreme! Remember, every natural living organism on this planet is a 100% raw-food eater.
They aren't 99% raw, they are 100% raw! That's trillion of organisms. Are they all being extreme? I think
not.

Also, as a general rule, the higher the water-con-
tent of the food, the higher its energy and vibration.
The lighter your diet, the more energy you will have.
To achieve your desired weight, stabilize the living-
water weight level in your body. One's living-water
weight will not stabilize until that last jump to a 100%
raw-diet (high in fruit and wild greens) is made.

Below are listed two special strategies I have
successfully employed to gain pounds of healthy
weight over the years. Employ them as part of your
daily dietary regime and you will see results.

Strategy 1: Coconuts and green juice

I have used the following formula to energize
my blood, build my body, and gain 25+ pounds of
healthy muscle weight (9+ kg):

I drink two to four coconuts worth of coconut
water daily. I typically buy young coconuts (with a
soft, jelly-like interior). I scoop out the jelly-like pulp
as a meal for myself (and my raw-foodist dog, Fenris).

Young coconuts are commonly found in Asian-food markets. I include with this program freshly-made green juice which saturates my body with usable muscle-building minerals.

This program targets the blood specifically. When you rebuild your blood, you rebuild your body. Coconut water is the breast-milk of Mother Earth. Coconut water is the closest substance to human blood plasma found in the plant world. 55% of the blood is plasma. Green chlorophyll is the closest substance to human hemoglobin in the plant world. Coconut water combined with green juice is a powerhouse way to revitalize the blood and build the body. Ann Wigmore often recommended coconut water mixed with wheatgrass juice, a combination I enjoy as well.

I eat the pulp inside the coco for its incredible raw plant fat content. Raw plant fats, as I mentioned before, are essential to a powerfully vibrant raw diet. Fats are much more important in the human diet than protein, and fats are also more important for body-building than protein. Raw plant fats lubricate the digestive tract, they are "soft" on the body (easy to assimilate), and they deliver specific protection to the wall of each cell. Fats also provide extra electrons to the cells and thus they are an anti-oxidant.

Here is my secret body-building formula that I drink almost every day:

"Captain's Powerhouse"

In a blender:
1 Young Coconut (Juice and Pulp)
1 Large Avocado
2 Handfuls of Wild or Organic Greens

Strategy 2: Eat only once or twice a day.

The following is another strategy you should employ to gain strength and muscular weight: Eat only once or twice a day. Eat large meals when you eat. Note: This is not necessarily the healthiest way to eat, but keep in mind what your goal is here -- to gain strength and healthy muscular weight. After you achieve your desired strength and weight, you can return to a more sustainable eating schedule. Here's an example for you: Though Sumo Wrestlers are big, fat, cooked-food eaters, the way they eat to gain weight is interesting and instructive. Sumo Wrestlers fast all day and then, right before they go to bed, they eat a massive cooked meal. What happens is the body "thinks" that there is a shortage of food all day so it conserves energy and the metabolism slows way down. Then, they eat a massive meal right before they go to sleep and the body is not able to process and assimilate most of the food -- so they inevitably gain weight (of course not healthy weight though!). It has been my experience that raw-foodists who eat all day are thinner than those who eat once or twice a day. For raw-eaters who eat all day, their bodies "think" that there is an abundance of food coming in so their metabolism speeds up in order to process all the food coming in.

To better illustrate this concept, I will use the following analogy: Anyone familiar with standard weight-training principles knows that to build mass you need to do low-repetition exercises with a heavy weight. And to tone-up, you need to do high-repetition exercises with a light weight. The same principles can be applied to eating for mass or eating to tone-up.

High-repetition exercises with a low weight equates to eating a high frequency of small meals throughout the day. You are not able to gain mass by eating this way. Low-repetition exercises with a high weight equates to eating a low frequency of large meals during the day (only one or two meals a day). This is by far the most important aspect of gaining weight and strength on The Raw-Food Diet.

In 1997, I took a 12-day trip to Hawaii. There were so many exotic fruits there, I found myself eating pretty much all day (high frequency of small meals). Guess what? I lost 13 pounds in those 12 days. When I returned home, I ate only at night and lifted weights and took in sunlight during the day and the weight returned quickly.

Chapter 4

Exercise And Weight Training

Total fitness has three vital components: Aerobic Conditioning, Flexibility, and Muscular Conditioning.

Aerobic activity is anything that uses up a lot of oxygen. Oxygen is delivered to the muscles by the cardiovascular system -- the lungs, heart, and circulation of the blood. The system is developed by continuous, high-repetition exercise such as running, swimming, jumping rope, riding a bicycle, etc.

Muscles, tendons, and ligaments tend to shorten over a period of time, which limits our range of motion and renders us more vulnerable to injury when sudden stresses are placed on these body parts. But we can counteract this tendency by stretching exercises and physical stretching programs.

The best way to develop and strengthen the muscles is resistance training. When you contract the muscles against resistance, they adapt to this level of effort. The best and most efficient way of doing this is through weight training.

To gain strength and muscular weight, do progressive, anaerobic exercise six days a week, giving yourself one day off. Push yourself -- be physical! And think *powerfully*. Remember, the Mind is the most important factor.

Both men and women can build beautiful sculpted muscles through intense resistance exercise. Remember, 50% of the body's weight is muscle.

Muscles, as their growth is promoted, provide the ground-work for genuine physical beauty. The more your muscles grow, the more beautiful you become. Bodily form and the perfect figure, can be developed by muscular development, sunshine on the skin, deep-breathing, and proper control of weight by eating naturally and sensibly. There is no other way to achieve and develop genuine physical beauty.

To improve your balance to an unimaginable level, lift weights standing up on one foot at a time. Experiment! You'll find that your form and lifting mechanics sharpen up dramatically.

Do the vigorous exercises you feel good doing. Do exercises which agree with you. You can exercise anywhere. Exercise whenever you watch television, listen to the radio, or audio tapes, etc. (but be on guard against the negative, hypnotic suggestion of mass media). Keep in mind that participating in mass media contributes to a negative attitude and a negative out-look on life, so avoid it whenever possible. When we were teenagers, David Wolfe, my brother Scott, and I used to pass a dumbbell back and forth while we watched a movie, doing sets of exercises until the movie was over!

To gain maximum weight and to build muscular size or strength, you must perform exercise feats which you are not presently capable of doing. You must attempt the momentarily impossible. Such attempts should involve maximum efforts against resistance. This is what separates success from failure.

Do exercises which are progressively stressful or resistant. Do exercises which are difficult yet safe, which you enjoy, and which suit your life-style. Preferably, exercise outdoors under the sun or, in the alternative, at a convenient facility. Exercise at a convenient time of day or night, as long and as frequently as possible, and as regularly as possible. Choose a program you will follow throughout your life. Exercise every part of your body as vigorously as possible. Be aware of each body part. Exercise until the resulting fatigue relaxes you.

Start your exercise program with amounts of weight and repetitions which are easy to perform. Advance gradually and increase it slowly. Muscles should be contracted to their fullest extent and joints should be carried through their full range of movement. Place demands on your body within reasonable limits. Once the muscles are warmed up, then conduct short periods of intense, vigorous, extremely-resistant exercise. This will put more muscle weight on your body than maintaining a long period of mild exercise.

To gain weight, do more anaerobic (without oxygen) exercises than aerobic exercises (with oxygen) in your workout. Aerobic exercise is good for your heart and helps you gain endurance, not muscular development.

A fantastic exercise is swimming underwater, or doing underwater laps in a pool. Swimming is an aerobic activity, but when you swim underwater while holding your breath, you greatly increase your lung capacity, which will help your weightlifting work-out. You will see a big difference in your breathing after a few weeks of doing the exercise consistently.

Aerobic exercises are light exercises such as: walking, jogging, long-distance running, dancing, long-distance swimming, long-distance cycling, cross-country skiing, etc.

To gain weight and develop muscles, do anaerobic exercises.

Anaerobic exercises are heavy exercises such

as: lifting heavy weights, low-repetition concentrated weight-lifting, arm-wrestling, sprinting, wrestling, rope climbing, jumping, speed cycling, sprint swimming, etc.

Anaerobic exercises are intense exercises which can only be tolerated for a few moments. They are short bursts of high-energy activities. They use muscle groups at high intensities which exceed the body's capacity to use oxygen to supply energy. They create an oxygen debt by using energy produced without oxygen. They are activities which demand such a great muscle explosion, the body has to rely upon an internal metabolic process for oxygen.

Breathe in-between each anaerobic exertion. Take deep, diaphragmatic breaths.

Anaerobic exercises may be: isotonic, isokinetic, isometric, and/or negative or "eccentric" exercises.

Isotonic exercise involves movement of a constant heavy weight through a full range of possible movement. It is a muscular action in which there is a change in the length of the muscle, while the tension remains constant. The bench press is a classic example of an isotonic exercise.

Isokinetic exercise is exercise in which there is accommodation resistance and constant speed.

Nautilus is a type of isokinetic machine where the machine varies the amount of resistance being lifted to match the force curve developed by the muscle. Isokinetics is exercising in which the maximum force of which the muscle is capable is applied throughout the range of motion.

Isometric exercise involves a static contraction. It is the application of a high percentage of your existing strength against an unmoving resistance, a fixed limit. Isometrics entails pushing against an immovable force such as: another set of opposing muscles, a wall, building, door, bar, taught rope, towel, two-ton truck, etc. If you push hard enough, you feel stress on your muscles. In isometrics, each exercise should be practiced at several joint angles. Training at many angles distributes the strength gains throughout the range of the muscle's movement. In isometrics, each "all-out" push or pull should be held as long as possible, to the point of muscular failure. Isometric exercises can be done practically anywhere. They are simple and effective. Isometrics increase the strength and improve the muscles' tone and shape. Isometric exercise entails muscular contraction where the muscle maintains a constant length and the joints do not move.

In negative or "eccentric" exercises, you lower the weight very slowly, at a smooth, steady pace, without interrupting the downward movement. In positive or "concentric" exercise, you raise the weight at normal speed. In negative exercise, your muscle is stretching and lengthening while maintaining tension against resistance. In positive exercise, the muscle is contracting and shortening against resistance. In negative exercise, you resist pressure and in positive exercise, you apply pressure. The muscle has the ability to handle more force during negative exercise than it can during positive exercise.

For example, when performing a bench press, the positive part of the repetition is the portion during which the weight is being pressed from the chest to arm's length. The negative portion of the repetition is the part during which the weight is lowered back down to the chest. In negative pull-ups, you climb into the top position using your legs, so that you simply lower yourself back down. Negative parallel bar dips can be done in the same way.

All four of these anaerobic exercise types: isotonic, isokinetic, isometric, and/or negative or "eccentric" should be employed as part of your workout. A sample workout would include: the military press (isotonic), lateral pull downs (isokinetic), pushing against a wall (isometric), and negative curls (eccentric), plus additional exercises.

Chapter 5

Sunshine

The human organism is solar-powered. All life on this spinning planet derives directly or indirectly from the Sun.

If you want to build muscle and strength, it is important to get out into the Sun. The Sun is the source of all Life on Earth. The Sun quickens the detoxification process and lays a solid foundation for healing and muscle-building by pulling toxins, in a magnetic fashion, out of the muscle tissue to the surface of the skin for elimination. The fact that humans have very little thick hair on the body clearly indicates we are designed for a naked life in the sunshine.

A common myth is that the sun causes skin cancer. The sun doesn't cause skin cancer, the sun causes all life on Earth! Skin cancer is caused by toxicity within the body. When this toxicity is detoxified through the skin (our largest eliminative organ), it is sometimes "baked" onto the skin, bringing forth a cancer condition. Blaming the Sun for skin cancer is like blaming fresh air for lung cancer. One thing causes cancer: A violation of the Laws of Nature.

What you must remember is that you must have internal protection from the Sun's rays in the form of proper, natural, raw-food nutrition. External "protection" like sunscreen is an abomination. The same internal mechanism that keeps a plant from burning up under the hot sun can keep you from sunburning. A plant is in direct sunlight for hours upon hours every day of its existence. A plant dries up and dies when it no longer has the internal protection that it requires.

Get in the Sun and get outside for exercise every day! You cannot gain strength and healthy weight if you are sitting indoors all day. The best place to exercise is not in an artificial, air-conditioned gym, but in the green outdoors among the living plants, wild animals, and fresh air. If you want to lift heavy weights, bring them outside and exercise in the open air with the sky above. If you feel you can do without them, do not wear shoes, gloves, or belts. Lift weights without clothing if possible. "Gymnasium" means "to train in the nude." However, always keep in mind your own safety when engaged in these activities.

Sunbathe and airbathe (get fresh, clean air over all the pores of your skin) in the nude. Sunlight and fresh air aid the nutritive processes of the body. You will never feel better than when your body is in shape and you have a deep-dark tan over all your skin. Thinness is associated with paleness. I have also found that people who are afraid of fruit are usually afraid of the Sun and afraid of exercise. So, eat fruit, get out in the Sun, and exercise!

When the body is warmed up by the Sun, the tissues expand. Thus, you may find in the summer it is easier to gain strength and weight under the hot summer Sun.

Chapter 6

Conclusions

Maintain your emotional poise. Release worry, fear, anxiety, jealousy, stress, nervousness, and neurosis through physical movement of the body, through the free flow of body energy, and through deep breathing. Take your aggressions out by engaging in anaerobic exercise.

Boxers, horse trainers, and successful athletes have long understood that abstinence from sex before a competition maintains strength. Overindulgence in sex with the resultant loss of nutrients during ejaculation, causes weight loss and energy depletion. After ejaculation, nutrients designed for other vital organs, are sidetracked into the production of reproductive materials. This depletion results in a momentary insufficiency in the nutrients available to other biological systems of the body. Sex is wonderful, but engage in sex at the appropriate times -- not before a work-out or contest!

Be true. Remember, half-measures never have and never will achieve the desired results. The only fools are those who fool themselves. I have a quote in my book **Nature's First Law: The Raw-Food Diet**

you should keep in mind: "The idea that natural nutrition may be followed by unnatural and harmful effects
is an absurd notion which should be abandoned once
and for all." Nutrition is no science -- it is very simple. Live by the Laws of Nature and you shall prosper;
live by the laws of civilization and you shall perish.
All weight loss and emaciation due to The Raw-Food
Diet is a result of the "good pushing out the bad" and
other catabolic detoxification processes. The strength
and weight will build if one is persistent.

The major problem that is plaguing humanity is
addiction. Addiction to toxicity; addiction to being in
a toxic physiological condition actually. People are
constantly trying to reach a level of euphoria artificial-
ly, which is theirs naturally. When you are 100% raw
for an extended period of time, it is a magical experience. Again, there is no magic pill, but there is a magic
process to achieving perfect health. If people would
just adhere to, and trust in, the Laws of Nature, they
could begin to realize their true potential, their life's
true meaning on this planet. Try it for yourself...and
you shall be convinced.

I eat exclusively raw plant foods to build my
body! Cooked food and other unnatural substances do
not build a body -- they destroy it. On the **Raw
Power! Video** in the Nature's First Law Catalog, I
show the audience different techniques on how to
become stronger with raw foods. On cooked foods, I

was on a plateau for years. When I went 100% raw, I unleashed a strength, balance, and energy that I never knew I had. The video contains my entire personal weekly exercise program. Check it out!

Appendix A:

Work-Outs

Men's Standard Work-Out

Monday / Wednesday / Friday

WARM-UP

<u>Neck Rolls</u>: 5 rolls to each side
<u>Side Bends</u>: 10 reps to each side
<u>Lunges/Achilles Stretches</u>: 5 combinations
<u>Windmills</u>: 20 reps to each side

CHEST

<u>Barbell Bench Press</u>: 5 sets + warm-up set
  1 set of 15 rep warm-up
  sets of 10,8,6,4,4 reps - stripping last two sets
<u>Incline Barbell Bench Press</u>: 5 sets
  sets of 10,8,6,4,4 reps - stripping last two sets
<u>Dumbbell Flys</u>: 5 sets
  sets of 10,8,8,8,6 reps
<u>Parallel Dips</u>: 5 sets
  sets of 15,10,8,8,8 reps
<u>Dumbbell Pullovers</u>: 3 sets
  sets of 15,15,15 reps

BACK

<u>Wide-Grip Chin-Ups</u>: 5 sets
  10 reps first 3 sets, go until failure last 2 sets
<u>Close-Grip Chin-Ups</u>: 5 sets
  10 reps each set
<u>T-Bar Rows</u>: 5 sets
  sets of 15,12,10,8,6 reps
<u>Bent-Over Barbell Rows</u>: 5 sets
  10 reps each set

THIGHS

<u>Squats</u>: 5 sets + warm-up set
  1 set of 20 rep warm-up
  sets of 10,8,6,4,4 reps
<u>Front Squats</u>: 4 sets
  sets of 10,8,8,6 reps
<u>Hack Squats</u>: 4 sets
  10 reps each set
<u>Lying Leg Curls</u>: 5 sets
  sets of 20,10,8,6,6 reps
<u>Standing Leg Curls</u>: 5 sets
  10 reps each set
<u>Straight-Leg Deadlifts</u>: 3 sets
  10 reps each set

CALVES

Donkey Calf Raises: 5 sets
  10 reps each set
Standing Calf Raises: 5 sets
  sets of 15,10,8,8,8 reps

ABDOMINALS

Bent-Knee Hanging Leg Raises: 100 reps
Bent-Over Twists: 100 reps each side
Crunches: 50 reps

CARDIOVASCULAR

Walk, Run, Bike, Swim, or Hike: 30-60 minutes

Tuesday / Thursday / Saturday

WARM-UP

Neck Rolls: 5 rolls to each side
Side Bends: 10 reps to each side
Lunges/Achilles Stretches: 5 combinations
Windmills: 20 reps to each side

SHOULDERS

Behind-Neck Barbell Presses: 4 sets + warm-up
  1 set of 15 rep warm-up
  sets of 10,8,8,6 reps

Dumbbell Lateral Raises: 5 sets
  8 reps each set
Bent-Over Lateral Raises: 5 sets
  8 reps each set
Dumbbell Shrugs: 3 sets
  10 reps each set

UPPER ARMS

Standing Barbell Curls: 5 sets
  sets of 15,10,8,6,4 reps
Incline Dumbbell Curls: 5 sets
  8 reps each set
Concentration Curls: 3 sets
  8 reps each set
Lying French Presses: 5 sets
  sets of 15,10,8,6,4 reps
Triceps Cable Pushdowns: 5 sets
  8 reps each set
One-Arm Triceps Extensions: 5 sets
  10 reps each set

FOREARMS

<u>Barbell Wrist Curls</u>: 5 sets
  10 reps each set
<u>Reverse Wrist Curls</u>: 3 sets
  10 reps each set

CALVES

<u>Seated Calf Raises</u>: 5 sets
  10 reps each set

ABDOMINALS

<u>Bent-Knee Sit-Ups</u>: 100 reps
<u>Incline Board Leg Raises</u>: 100 reps

CARDIOVASCULAR

<u>Walk, Run, Bike, Swim, or Hike</u>: 30-60 minutes

Men's Advanced Work-Out

Monday / Wednesday / Friday

WARM-UP

<u>Neck Rolls</u>: 5 rolls to each side
<u>Side Bends</u>: 10 reps to each side
<u>Lunges/Achilles Stretches</u>: 5 combinations
<u>Windmills</u>: 20 reps to each side

ABDOMINALS

<u>Roman Chair Sit-Ups</u>: 5 minutes

CHEST & BACK

Superset:
<u>Barbell Bench Press</u>: 5 sets + warm-up set
  1 set of 15 rep warm-up
  sets of 10,8,6,4,4 reps
<u>Wide-Grip Chin-Ups</u>: 5 sets
  10 reps each set

Superset:
<u>Dumbbell Incline Presses</u>: 5 sets
  sets of 10,8,8,8,6 reps
<u>Close-Grip Chin-Ups</u>: 5 sets
  10 reps each set

Dumbbell Flys: 5 sets
  sets of 10,8,8,8,6 reps
Parallel Dips: 5 sets
  sets of 15,10,8,8,8 reps
T-Bar Rows: 5 sets
  sets of 15,10,8,8,8 reps
Bent-Over Barbell Rows: 5 sets
  10 reps each set

Superset:
Seated Cable Rows: 5 sets
  10 reps each set
Dumbbell Pullovers: 5 sets
  15 reps each set

THIGHS

Squats: 6 sets
  sets of 15,10,8,8,6,4 reps
Front Squats: 4 sets
  sets of 10,8,8,6 reps

Superset:
Hack Squats: 5 sets + warm up set
  1 set of 15 rep warm-up
  sets of 10,8,8,8,8 reps
Lying Leg Curls: 5 sets + warm-up set
  1 set of 15 rep warm-up
  sets of 10,8,8,8,8 reps

Superset:
Standing Leg Curls: 5 sets
　10 reps each set
Straight-Leg Deadlifts: 5 sets
　10 reps each set

CALVES

Donkey Calf Raises: 5 sets
　10 reps each set
Standing Calf Raises: 5 sets
　10 reps each set
Seated Calf Raises: 5 sets
　10 reps each set

ABDOMINALS

Bent-Knee Hanging Leg Raises: 150 reps
Crunches: 150 reps
Bent-Over Twists: 100 reps each side

CARDIOVASCULAR

Walk, Run, Bike, Swim, or Hike: 30-60 minutes

Tuesday / Thursday / Saturday

WARM-UP

Neck Rolls: 5 rolls to each side

Side Bends: 10 reps to each side
Lunges/Achilles Stretches: 5 combinations
Windmills: 20 reps to each side

ABDOMINALS

Roman Chair Sit-Ups: 5 minutes

SHOULDERS

Superset:
Behind-Neck Barbell Presses: 5 sets + warm-up set
  1 set of 15 rep warm-up
  sets of 10,8,8,8,6 reps
Dumbbell Lateral Raises: 5 sets
  8 reps each set

Superset:
Machine Front Press: 5 sets
  8 reps each set
Bent-Over Lateral Raises: 5 sets
  8 reps each set

Superset:
Upright Rows: 5 sets
  10 reps each set
One-Arm Seated Cable Laterals: 5 sets
  10 reps each set, each arm

UPPER ARMS

Superset:
Standing Barbell Curls: 5 sets
  sets of 15,10,8,6,4 reps
Lying French Presses: 5 sets
  sets of 15,10,8,6,4 reps

Superset:
Alternate Dumbbell Curls: 5 sets
  8 reps each set
Triceps Cable Pushdowns: 5 sets
  8 reps each set

Superset:
Concentration Curls: 5 sets
  8 reps each set
One-Arm Triceps Extensions: 5 sets
  12 reps each set

Reverse Push-Ups: 5 sets
  15 reps each set

FOREARMS

Superset:
Barbell Wrist Curls: 5 sets
  10 reps each set
Reverse Wrist Curls: 5 sets
  10 reps each set

One-Arm Wrist Curls: 5 sets
  10 reps each set

CALVES

Standing Calf Raises: 5 sets
  sets of 15,10,8,8,8 reps
Calf Raises On Leg Press Machine: 5 sets
  10 reps each set

ABDOMINALS

Bent-Knee Sit-Ups: 150 reps
Incline Board Leg Raises: 150 reps
Side Leg Raises: 100 reps each side
Hyperextensions: 3 set
  10 reps each set

CARDIOVASCULAR

Walk, Run, Bike, Swim, or Hike: 30-60 minutes

Women's Standard Work-Out

Monday / Wednesday / Friday

WARM-UP

Neck Rolls: 5 rolls to each side
Side Bends: 10 reps to each side
Lunges/Achilles Stretches: 5 combinations
Windmills: 20 reps to each side

CHEST

Barbell Bench Press: 4 sets + warm-up set
  1 set of 15 rep warm-up
  sets of 12,10,8,6 reps
Incline Barbell Bench Press: 4 sets
  sets of 12,10,8,8 reps
Dumbbell Flys: 4 sets
  sets of 10,8,8,8 reps
Dumbbell Pullovers: 3 sets
  sets of 12,12,12 reps

BACK

Lat Machine Pulldowns: 4 sets
  sets of 15,12,10,8 reps
Lat Machine Pulldowns - Close-Grip: 4 sets
  sets of 15,12,10,8 reps

<u>Bent-Over Barbell Rows</u>: 3 sets
  10 reps each set

THIGHS

<u>Squats</u>: 3 sets + warm-up set
  1 set of 20 rep warm-up
  sets of 12,10,8 reps
<u>Hack Squats</u>: 4 sets
  10 reps each set
<u>Lying Leg Curls</u>: 5 sets
  sets of 20,10,8,6,6 reps
<u>Standing Leg Curls</u>: 5 sets
  10 reps each set

CALVES

<u>Standing Calf Raises</u>: 5 sets
  sets of 15,10,8,8,8 reps

ABDOMINALS

<u>Bent-Knee Hanging Leg Raises</u>: 50 reps
<u>Bent-Over Twists</u>: 100 reps each side
<u>Crunches</u>: 100 reps

CARDIOVASCULAR

<u>Walk, Run, Bike, Swim, or Hike</u>: 30-60 minutes

Tuesday / Thursday / Saturday

WARM-UP

<u>Neck Rolls</u>: 5 rolls to each side
<u>Side Bends</u>: 10 reps to each side
<u>Lunges/Achilles Stretches</u>: 5 combinations
<u>Windmills</u>: 20 reps to each side

SHOULDERS

<u>Behind-Neck Barbell Presses</u>: 4 sets + warm-up
  1 set of 15 rep warm-up
  sets of 12,10,8,8 reps
<u>Dumbbell Lateral Raises</u>: 4 sets
  8 reps each set
<u>Bent-Over Lateral Raises</u>: 4 sets
  8 reps each set
<u>Dumbbell Shrugs</u>: 3 sets
  10 reps each set

UPPER ARMS

<u>Standing Barbell Curls</u>: 4 sets
  sets of 12,10,8,6 reps
<u>Incline Dumbbell Curls</u>: 4 sets
  8 reps each set
<u>Concentration Curls</u>: 3 sets
  8 reps each set

Lying French Presses: 4 sets
  sets of 12,10,8,6 reps
Triceps Cable Pushdowns: 4 sets
  8 reps each set
One-Arm Triceps Extensions: 3 sets
  10 reps each set

FOREARMS

Barbell Wrist Curls: 4 sets
  10 reps each set
Reverse Wrist Curls: 3 sets
  10 reps each set

CALVES

Seated Calf Raises: 4 sets
  10 reps each set

ABDOMINALS

Bent-Knee Sit-Ups: 100 reps
Incline Board Leg Raises: 50 reps

CARDIOVASCULAR

Walk, Run, Bike, Swim, or Hike: 30-60 minutes

Women's Advanced Work-Out

Monday / Wednesday / Friday

WARM-UP

Neck Rolls: 5 rolls to each side
Side Bends: 10 reps to each side
Lunges/Achilles Stretches: 5 combinations
Windmills: 20 reps to each side

ABDOMINALS

Roman Chair Sit-Ups: 5 minutes

CHEST & BACK

Superset:
Barbell Bench Press: 5 sets + warm-up set
   1 set of 15 rep warm-up
   sets of 12,10,8,6,4 reps
Lat Machine Pulldowns: 5 sets
   sets of 12,10,8,8,6 reps

Superset:
Dumbbell Incline Presses: 5 sets
   sets of 12,10,8,8,6 reps
Lat Machine Pulldowns - Close Grip: 5 sets
   sets of 12,10,8,8,6 reps

Dumbbell Flys: 5 sets
  sets of 10,8,8,8,6 reps
Parallel Dips: 5 sets
  sets of 15,10,8,8,8 reps
Bent-Over Barbell Rows: 5 sets
  10 reps each set

Superset:
Seated Cable Rows: 5 sets
  10 reps each set
Dumbbell Pullovers: 5 sets
  15 reps each set

THIGHS

Squats: 6 sets
  sets of 15,10,8,8,6,6 reps
Front Squats: 4 sets
  sets of 10,8,8,6 reps

Superset:
Hack Squats: 5 sets + warm up set
  1 set of 15 rep warm-up
  sets of 10,8,8,8,8 reps
Lying Leg Curls: 5 sets + warm-up set
  1 set of 15 rep warm-up
  sets of 10,8,8,8,8 reps

Superset:
Standing Leg Curls: 5 sets
  10 reps each set
Straight-Leg Deadlifts: 5 sets
  10 reps each set

CALVES

Standing Calf Raises: 5 sets
  10 reps each set
Seated Calf Raises: 5 sets
  10 reps each set

ABDOMINALS

Bent-Knee Hanging Leg Raises: 100 reps
Crunches: 150 reps
Bent-Over Twists: 100 reps each side

CARDIOVASCULAR

Walk, Run, Bike, Swim, or Hike: 30-60 minutes

Tuesday / Thursday / Saturday

WARM-UP

Neck Rolls: 5 rolls to each side
Side Bends: 10 reps to each side
Lunges/Achilles Stretches: 5 combinations

Windmills: 20 reps to each side

ABDOMINALS

Roman Chair Sit-Ups: 5 minutes

SHOULDERS

Superset:
Behind-Neck Barbell Presses: 5 sets + warm-up set
  1 set of 15 rep warm-up
  sets of 10,8,8,8,6 reps
Dumbbell Lateral Raises: 5 sets
  8 reps each set

Superset:
Machine Front Press: 5 sets
  8 reps each set
Bent-Over Lateral Raises: 5 sets
  8 reps each set

Superset:
Upright Rows: 5 sets
  10 reps each set
One-Arm Seated Cable Laterals: 5 sets
  10 reps each set, each arm

UPPER ARMS

Superset:
<u>Standing Barbell Curls</u>: 5 sets
  sets of 15,10,8,6,6 reps
<u>Lying French Presses</u>: 5 sets
  sets of 15,10,8,6,6 reps

Superset:
<u>Alternate Dumbbell Curls</u>: 5 sets
  8 reps each set
<u>Triceps Cable Pushdowns</u>: 5 sets
  8 reps each set

Superset:
<u>Concentration Curls</u>: 5 sets
  8 reps each set
<u>One-Arm Triceps Extensions</u>: 5 sets
  12 reps each set

<u>Reverse Push-Ups</u>: 5 sets
  15 reps each set

FOREARMS

Superset:
<u>Barbell Wrist Curls</u>: 5 sets
  10 reps each set
<u>Reverse Wrist Curls</u>: 5 sets
  10 reps each set

One-Arm Wrist Curls: 5 sets
  10 reps each set

CALVES

Standing Calf Raises: 5 sets
  sets of 15,10,8,8,8 reps
Calf Raises On Leg Press Machine: 5 sets
  10 reps each set

ABDOMINALS

Bent-Knee Sit-Ups: 150 reps
Incline Board Leg Raises: 150 reps
Side Leg Raises: 100 reps each side
Hyperextensions: 3 set
  10 reps each set

CARDIOVASCULAR

Walk, Run, Bike, Swim, or Hike: 30-60 minutes

Over 50 Work-Out (Men & Women)

Monday / Thursday

WARM-UP

Neck Rolls: 5 rolls to each side
Side Bends: 10 reps to each side
Lunges/Achilles Stretches: 5 combinations
Windmills: 20 reps to each side

CHEST

Barbell Bench Press: 3 sets + warm-up set
  1 set of 15 rep warm-up
  sets of 12,10,8 reps
Incline Barbell Bench Press: 3 sets
  sets of 12,10,8 reps
Dumbbell Flys: 3 sets
  sets of 12,10,8 reps
Dumbbell Pullovers: 3 sets
  12 reps each set

BACK

Lat Machine Pulldowns: 3 sets
  10 reps each set
Lat Machine Pulldowns - Close-Grip: 3 sets
  10 reps each set

Bent-Over Barbell Rows: 3 sets
  10 reps each set

THIGHS

Freehand Squats: 3 sets
  12 reps each set
Hack Squats: 3 sets
  sets of 12,10,8 reps
Lying Leg Curls: 3 sets
  sets of 15,12,10 reps
Standing Leg Curls: 3 sets
  10 reps each set

CALVES

Standing Calf Raises: 4 sets
  sets of 15,12,10,8 reps

ABDOMINALS

Bent-Over Twists: 50 reps each side
Crunches: 50 reps

CARDIOVASCULAR

Walk, Run, Bike, Swim, or Hike: 30-60 minutes

Tuesday / Friday

WARM-UP

Neck Rolls: 5 rolls to each side
Side Bends: 10 reps to each side
Lunges/Achilles Stretches: 5 combinations
Windmills: 20 reps to each side

SHOULDERS

Behind-Neck Barbell Presses: 3 sets + warm-up
 1 set of 15 rep warm-up
 sets of 12,10,8 reps
Dumbbell Lateral Raises: 3 sets
 12 reps each set
Dumbbell Shrugs: 3 sets
 10 reps each set

UPPER ARMS

Standing Barbell Curls: 3 sets
 sets of 15,12,10 reps
Concentration Curls: 3 sets
 10 reps each set
Triceps Cable Pushdowns: 3 sets
 10 reps each set

FOREARMS

<u>Barbell Wrist Curls</u>: 3 sets
  10 reps each set
<u>Reverse Wrist Curls</u>: 3 sets
  10 reps each set

CALVES

<u>Seated Calf Raises</u>: 4 sets
  sets of 15,12,10,8 reps

ABDOMINALS

<u>Bent-Knee Sit-Ups</u>: 50 reps
<u>Incline Board Leg Raises</u>: 50 reps

CARDIOVASCULAR

<u>Walk, Run, Bike, Swim, or Hike</u>: 30-60 minutes

Wednesday / Saturday

WARM-UP

<u>Neck Rolls</u>: 5 rolls to each side
<u>Side Bends</u>: 10 reps to each side
<u>Lunges/Achilles Stretches</u>: 5 combinations
<u>Windmills</u>: 20 reps to each side

ABDOMINALS

Bent-Over Twists: 50 reps each side
Crunches: 50 reps
Bent-Knee Sit-Ups: 50 reps
Incline Board Leg Raises: 50 reps

CARDIOVASCULAR

Walk, Run, Bike, Swim, or Hike: 60-90 minutes

Appendix B:

Definition Of Terms And
Proper Execution Of Exercises

<u>Aerobic Exercise</u>: With oxygen. The demands of muscles for oxygen are met by the circulation of oxygen in the blood. Examples are: walking, swimming, long-distance running, etc.

<u>Alternate Dumbbell Curls</u>: Stand upright, a dumbbell in each hand hanging at arm's length. Curl one weight forward and up, holding your elbow steady at your waist and twisting your wrist slightly, bringing the thumb down and little finger up. Curl the weight as high as you can, then bring it back down under control through the same arc. Switch arms and repeat.

<u>Anaerobic Exercise</u>: Without oxygen. The oxygen demands of the muscles are so high that the circulatory system cannot supply adequate oxygen. Examples are: weight-lifting, sprinting, arm-wrestling, etc.

<u>Barbell</u>: A long bar with weights at both ends, designed to be used by both hands at once.

<u>Barbell Bench Press</u>: Lie on a flat bench, your feet on the floor for balance. Your grip should be wide

enough so that as you lower the bar to your chest, your forearms should point straight up. Lift the bar off the rack and hold it at arm's length above you. Lower the bar slowly until it touches just below your pectoral muscles. The bar should come to a complete stop at this point. Press the bar upward until your arms are fully locked out.

Barbell Wrist Curls: Take hold of a barbell with an underhand grip, hands close together. Straddle a bench with your forearms resting on the bench but with your wrists and hands hanging over the end, elbows and wrists the same distance apart. Lock your knees in against your elbows to stabilize them. Bend your wrists and lower the weight toward the floor. When you can't lower the bar any further, carefully open your fingers a little bit and let the weight roll down out of the palms of your hands. Roll the weight back into the palms of your hands, contract the forearms, and lift the weight as high as you can without letting your forearms come up off the bench.

Behind-Neck Barbell Presses: Sitting on a seated press bench, lift the barbell overhead (this is your starting position). Lower the bar behind your head slowly, letting the bar slightly touch your shoulders. Press the weight straight up to the starting position, keeping your elbows as far back as possible during the movement.

Bent-Knee Hanging Leg Raises: Take hold of a chin-up bar with an overhand grip and hang at arm's length from the bar. Bend your knees, then lift your legs as high as possible. Lower them back to the starting position. Do not swing while performing this exercise.

Bent-Knee Sit-Ups: Lie on your back, knees bent, feet flat on the floor, your hands on the outside of your thighs. Sit up and bring your head as close to your knees as possible. Lower yourself slowly back to the floor. Do this exercise slowly and always keep your chin pressed to your chest.

Bent-Over Barbell Rows: Standing with your feet a few inches apart, grasp the bar with a wide, overhand grip. With your knees slightly bent, bend forward until your upper body is about parallel to the floor. Keep your back straight and let the bar hang at arm's length below you, almost touching the shinbone. Lift the bar upward until it touches the upper abdominals, then slowly lower it again to the starting position.

Bent-Over Lateral Raises: Sit on the end of a bench, knees together, and take a dumbbell in each hand. Bend forward from the waist and bring the dumbbells together behind your calves. Turn your hands so that your palms face one another. Keeping your body steady, lift the weights out to either side, turning your wrists so that the thumbs are lower than the little fingers. With your arms slightly bent, lift the dumbbells to a point just higher than your head, then, keeping your knees together, lower them again slowly to behind your calves, resisting all the way down.

<u>Bent-Over Twists</u>: Stand upright, legs straight, feet shoulder width apart. Hold a broom handle across the back of your shoulders. Bend forward from the waist as far as comfortable. Turning from the waist but not letting the hips move at all, twist in one direction until the end of the broom handle is pointing toward the floor. Continue this windmill movement, swinging first in one direction, then back in the other direction.

<u>Calf Raises On Leg Press Machine</u>: Using a leg press machine, position yourself as if to do a leg press, only push against the foot pads with your toes, leaving your heels unsupported. Press the weight upward with your toes until fully extended, then let your toes come back toward you, feeling the fullest possible stretch in the calf muscles.

<u>Cardiovascular Training</u>: Cardiovascular training is an integral part of overall conditioning. These exercises strengthen the heart, lungs, and circulatory system. See *Aerobic Exercise*.

<u>Close-Grip Chin-Ups</u>: Take hold of the chin-up bar with your hands close together in an underhand grip. Pull yourself up, lean your head slightly back so that

your chest nearly touches your hands. Lower your body back to the starting position.

Concentration Curls: In a standing position, bend over slightly and take a dumbbell in one hand. Rest your free arm on your knee to stabilize yourself. Curl the weight up to the deltoid without moving the upper arm or the elbow. Lower the weight slowly, resisting all the way down to full extension.

Crunches: Lie on your back on the floor. With your knees bent, raise your legs and place your feet against a wall or bench for support. Place your fingertips on your temples. Raise your head and shoulders toward your knees with a sit-up motion and simultaneously lift the pelvis and feel the contraction of the abdominals as the upper and lower body crunch together. Flex the abdominals to get the fullest possible contraction.

Donkey Calf Raises: Place your toes on a block, bend forward from the waist, and lean on a bench or table for support. Your toes should be directly below your hips. Have your training partner add resistance by seating her/himself across your hips, as far back as possible to keep pressure off the lower back. Lower your heels as far as possible, then come back up on your toes until your calves are fully contracted.

Dumbbell: A short bar with weights at both ends, intended for use by one hand at a time.

Dumbbell Flys: Lie on a bench holding dumbbells at arm's length above you, palms facing one another. Lower the weights out and down to either side in a wide arc as far as you can, feeling the pectoral muscles stretch to their maximum. The palms should remain facing each other throughout the movement. Bring the weights to a complete stop at a lower point than the bench, then lift them back up to the starting position along the same wide arc.

Dumbbell Incline Presses: Take a dumbbell in each hand and lie down on an incline bench. Lift the dumbbells to shoulder height, palms facing forward (this is your starting position). Press them simultaneously straight up overhead, then lower them back to the starting position. Vary the angle of the incline from workout to workout, or from set from set in the same workout.

Dumbbell Lateral Raises: Take a dumbbell in each hand, bend forward slightly, and bring the weights together in front of you at arm's length. Lift the weights out and up to either side, turning your wrists slightly so that the rear of the dumbbell is higher than the front. Lift the weights to a point slightly higher than your shoulders, then lower them slowly, resisting all the way down.

Dumbbell Pullovers: Lie across a bench with your feet flat on the floor. Place a dumbbell on the floor behind your head. Reach back and grasp the weight. Keeping your arms bent, raise the weight and bring it just over your head to your chest. Lower the weight slowly back to the starting position without touching the floor, feeling the lats stretch out to their fullest.

Dumbbell Shrugs: Stand upright, arms at sides, with a heavy dumbbell in each hand. Raise your shoulders as high as you can, as if trying to touch them to your ears. Hold at the top for a moment, then release and return to the starting position. Try not to move anything but your shoulders.

Freehand Squats: Stand straight up, flat-footed, arms crossed over your chest. Head up, back straight, feet 16 inches apart. Squat until upper thighs are parallel to floor. Return to starting position. Inhale down, exhale up.

Front Squats: Step up to the rack, bring your arms up under the bar, keeping the elbows high, cross your arms and grasp the bar with your hands to control it. Then lift the weight off the rack. Step back and separate your feet for balance. Bend your knees and, keeping your head up and your back straight, lower yourself until your thighs are below parallel to the floor. Push yourself back up to the starting position.

Hack Squats: Hook your shoulders under the padded bars. Your feet should be together, toes pointed slight-

ly out. Press downward with your legs and lift the
mechanism, stopping when your legs are fully extended. Bend your knees and lower yourself all the way
down. Push yourself back up to the starting position.

Hyperextensions: Position yourself face down across
a hyperextension bench, with your heels hooked under
the rear supports. Clasp your hands across your chest
or behind your head and bend forward and down as far
as possible, feeling the lower back muscles stretch.
From this position, come back up until your torso is
just above parallel.

Incline Barbell Bench Press: Lie back on an incline
bench. Reach up and grasp the bar with a medium-
wide grip. Lift the bar off the rack and hold it straight
overhead, arms locked. Lower the weight down to the
upper chest, stop for a moment, then press it back up
to the starting position.

Incline Board Leg Raises: Lie on your back on an
incline board, head higher than your feet. Reach back
and take hold of the top of the board or some other
support. Keeping your legs straight and feet flexed,
raise them up as high as you can, then lower them
slowly, stopping just as they touch the board.
Breathing is very important while doing this exercise.
As you raise your legs and compress the abdominal
cavity, breathe out; as you lower your legs again,

inhale deeply. Keep your chin tucked forward into the chest.

Incline Dumbbell Curls: Sit back on an incline bench holding a dumbbell in each hand. Keeping your elbows well forward throughout the movement, curl the weights forward and up to shoulder level. Lower the weights again, fully under control, and pause at the bottom to keep from swinging the weights up on the next repetition.

Lat Machine Pulldowns: Sit on the seat of a Lat Machine. Using a long bar, grasp it with a wide, over-hand grip with your knees hooked under the support. Pull the bar down smoothly until it touches the back of your neck, making the upper back do the work. Release, extend the arms again, and feel the lats fully stretch.

Lat Machine Pulldowns - Close Grip: Sit on the seat of a Lat Machine. Grasp the bar with a close, under-hand grip, your hands about 10 inches apart, with your knees hooked under the support. Pull the bar down smoothly until your hands slightly touch the top of your chest. Release, extend the arms again, and feel the lats fully stretch.

Lunges/Achilles Stretches: From a standing position with your feet together, step forward as far as you can with the left foot, keeping both feet pointed straight ahead. Bend your left knee and lower yourself as far as you can, keeping your back and your right leg straight. Put your hands down on either side of the forward foot for balance. Push up with your hands and straighten the left leg, but stay bent over with your hands remaining by your left foot. Keep both feet in place and flat on the floor, feeling the stretch in the back of your left leg and the Achilles' tendon of your right. Bend your head down as close as possible to the left knee. Slowly stand up and switch sides.

Lying Leg Curls: Lie face downward on a Leg Curl machine and hook your heels under the lever mechanism. Your legs should be stretched out straight. Keeping flat on the bench, curl your legs up as far as possible, until the leg biceps are fully contracted. Release and slowly lower the weight back to the starting position.

Lying Triceps Extensions: Lie along a bench, your head just off the end with knees bent and feet flat on the bench. Take hold of an E-Z bar with an overhand grip, hands about 10 inches apart. Press the weight up until your arms are locked out, but not straight up over your face (this is your starting position). Instead, the weight should be back behind the top of your head, with your triceps doing the work of holding it there. Keeping your elbows stationary, lower the weight down toward your forehead, then press it back up to the starting position, stopping just short of vertical.

Machine Front Press: Grasp the bar at shoulder level and press upward until your arms are locked out, then come back down slowly to the starting position, going through the longest range of motion possible.

Neck Rolls: Stand upright, hands at your sides. Breathe deeply, letting your shoulders, arms, and whole body relax as much as possible. Slowly rotate your head and neck to the left one complete circle. After one complete rotation to the left, do another one all the way around to the right.

One-Arm Seated Cable Laterals: Sitting on a stool or low bench, take hold of a handle attached to a floor-level pulley in such a way that your arm is fully extended across the front of your body. Keeping your body as still as possible, pull the handle across and up until your arm is fully extended to the side at about shoulder height. Lower the weight back to the starting position.

One-Arm Triceps Extensions: Sitting on a bench, take a dumbbell in one hand and hold it extended overhead. Keeping your elbow stationary and close to your head, lower the dumbbell down in an arc behind your head as far as you can. Feel the triceps stretch to their fullest, then press the weight back up to the starting position.

One-Arm Wrist Curls: Take hold of a dumbbell with

one arm and sit on a bench. Lean forward and place your forearm on your thigh so that your wrist and the weight extend out over the knee, with your palm and the inside of your forearm facing upward. Bend forward, reach over with your free hand, and take hold of the elbow of the working arm to stabilize it. Bend your wrist and lower the weight as far as possible toward the floor, opening your fingers slightly to let the dumbbell roll down out of your palm. Close your fingers again and curl the weight up as high as you can. Finish repetitions, switch arms and repeat.

Parallel Dips: Taking hold of the parallel bars, raise yourself up and lock out your arms. As you bend your elbows and lower yourself between the bars, try to stay as upright as possible. From the bottom of the movement, press yourself back up until your arms are locked out, then flex pectorals and triceps to increase contraction.

Repetition (rep): One complete exercise movement, from starting position, through the full range of movement, then back to the beginning.

Reverse Push-Ups: Place a bench behind your back and hold onto the bench at its edge, hands about shoulder width apart. Place your heels on another bench at a level higher than the bench you are holding on to. Bending your elbows, lower your body as far as you can toward the floor. Then push back up, locking out your arms to work the upper triceps. Also known as "Bench Dips."

Reverse Wrist Curls: Grasp a barbell with an overhand grip, hands about 10 inches apart. Lay your forearms on top of your thighs so that they are parallel to the floor and your wrists and hands are free and unsupported. Bend your wrists forward and lower the bar as far as you can. Then bring them back up and lift the bar as far as possible, trying not to let the forearms move during the exercise.

Roman Chair Sit-Ups: Sit on the Roman Chair bench, hook your feet under the support, and fold your arms in front of you. Keeping your stomach tucked in, lower yourself to approximately a 70-degree angle. Raise yourself back up and come forward as far as possible, deliberately flexing and "crunching" your abdominal muscles to increase the contraction.

Seated Cable Rows: Take hold of the handles and sit with your feet braced against the crossbar, knees slightly bent. Extend your arms and bend forward slightly, feeling the lats stretch. From this beginning position, pull the handles back toward your body and touch them to your abdomen, feeling the back muscles doing most of the work. Your back should arch, your chest stick out, and try to touch the shoulder blades together as you draw the weight toward you. When the handles touch your abdomen you should be sitting upright. Keeping the weight under control, release and let the handles go forward again, once more stretching out the lats.

Seated Calf Raises: Sit on the machine and place your toes on the bottom crosspiece, hooking your knees under the crossbar. Slowly lower your heels as far toward the ground as possible, then press back up on your toes until your calves are fully contracted. Use a steady, rhythmic motion.

Set: A group of repetitions (reps). The number is arbitrary. Programs designed to produce cardiovascular fitness generally use high-repetition sets, while those that aim for strength use fewer repetitions.

Side Bends: Stand upright, feet very wide apart. Raise your right hand high overhead, and put your left hand down on the side of your left leg. Stretch upward with your right arm as high as you can, and then begin bending to your left, continuing the stretch, and sliding your left hand down your left leg for support. Hold for count of 5, then slowly return to starting position. Lower your right arm, raise your left, and repeat the Side Bend to your right.

Side Leg Raises: Lie on your side supporting yourself on your elbow, your lower leg bent under for support. Keeping the upper leg straight, raise it slowly as high as it will go, then lower it again, but stopping short of letting it touch the floor. Don't move your hips at all during this movement.

Squats: With the barbell on a rack, step under it so that it rests across the back of your shoulders, hold on to the bar to balance it, raise up to lift it off the rack, and step away. Keeping your head up and your back straight, bend your knees and lower yourself until your thighs are just lower than parallel to the floor. From this point, push yourself back up to the starting position.

Standing Barbell Curls: Stand with feet a few inches apart and grasp the bar with an underhanded grip, hands about shoulder width apart. Let the bar hang down at arm's length in front of you. Curl the bar out and up in a wide arc and bring it up as high as you can, your elbows close to the body and stationary. Lower the weight, following the same arc and resisting the weight all the way down until your arms are fully extended.

Standing Calf Raises: Stand with your toes on the block of a standing Calf Raise machine, your heels extended out into space. Hook your shoulders under the pads and straighten your legs, lifting the weight clear of the support. Lower your heels as far as possible toward the floor, keeping your knees slightly bent throughout the movement in order to work the lower area of the calves as well as the upper, and feeling the calf muscles stretch to the maximum. From the bottom of the movement, come up on your toes as far as possible.

Standing Leg Curls: Stand against the machine and hook one leg behind the lever mechanism. Hold yourself steady and curl the leg up as high as possible. Release and slowly lower the weight back to the starting position. Switch legs and repeat.

Straight-Leg Deadlifts: Place a barbell on the floor in front of you. Bend your knees, lean forward, and grasp the bar in a medium-wide grip, one hand in an overhand grip, the other in an underhand grip. Try to keep your back straight. Begin the lift by driving with your legs. Straighten up until you are standing upright, then throw the chest out and the shoulders back as if coming to attention. Keep your legs locked and bend forward from the waist, your back straight, until your torso is about parallel to the floor, the bar hanging at arm's length below you. Straighten up again, pull your shoulders back, and arch your back.

Stripping: The act of removing some weights from the bar at the end of a set in order to squeeze out a few more reps that otherwise would not have been possible using the heavy weight originally put on the bar.

Superset: A set of two or more exercises performed in a row without stopping (zero rest).

T-Bar Rows: Standing on a block with your feet close together, knees slightly bent, bend down and grasp the handles of the T-Bar machine with an overhand grip. Straighten your legs slightly and lift up until your body is at about a 45-degree angle. Without changing this angle, lift the weight up until it touches your chest, then lower it again to arm's length, keeping the weight off the floor.

Triceps Cable Pushdowns: Hook a bar to an overhead cable and pulley, stand close to the bar and grasp it with an overhand grip, hands about 10 inches apart. Keep your elbows tucked in close to your body and stationary. Press the bar down as far as possible, locking out your arms and feeling the triceps contract fully. Release and let the bar come up as far as possible without moving the elbows.

Upright Rows: Stand grasping a barbell with an overhand grip, hands a few inches apart. Let the bar hang down in front of you. Lift it straight up, keeping it close to your body, until the bar just about touches your chin. From the top, lower it once more under control to the starting position.

Wide-Grip Chin-Ups: Take hold of the chin-up bar with an overhand grip, hands as wide apart as practicable. Hang from the bar, then pull yourself up so that the back of your neck touches the bar. Hold for a brief

moment, then lower yourself slowly back to the starting position.

  Windmills: Stay in the bent-over position, straighten
your arms out to each side, and twist so that you touch
your right hand to your left foot. Your left arm should
remain straight and end up pointing at the sky. At the
same time, turn your head so that you are looking up
behind you. Repeat the movement to the other side,
touching your left hand to your right foot.

Appendix C:

Body-Building Recipes

All the ingredients in the following recipes are 100% raw, organic, & vegan. Do your best to never eat outside of these guidelines. All of the following recipes have proven to be very effective for me and people I've worked with in building and maintaining a super-strong and healthy body. You may find that some of these recipes don't follow proper food-combining principles. For the most part, the commonly-known food-combining principles were formulated by and for cooked-food eaters -- they don't pertain to you. However, each food has its own nutritional make-up and fermentation rate. So, if you find that a certain recipe does not agree with you and you experience intestinal discomfort, simply switch to another recipe. Some of these body-building recipes require a juicer or blender. I highly recommend the Green Power Juicer, the Commercial Champion Juicer, the Miracle Wheatgrass Juicer, and the Vita-Mix Blender. These are all great appliances, I personally own them all. To order these products, please call Nature's First Law at 1-800-205-2350.

Nori Rolls

6-8 Raw, Sun-Dried Nori Sheets
2 Cups Soaked Sunflower Seeds
1 Cup Soaked Almonds
2 Carrots
3 Large Avocados
1/2 Head Green Leaf Lettuce
2 Handfuls Sunflower Sprouts (with green leaves)
2 Cups Shredded Zucchini
1 Cup Shredded Red Cabbage

Soak sunflower seeds and almonds separately for 8-10 hours and rinse. Alternate putting the sunflower seeds, almonds, and carrots through a Champion or Green Power Juicer and into a bowl. Use the blank plate for the juicer, a paté-like mixture will come out of the juicer. Mix until even. Spread sunflower sprouts, lettuce, zucchini, cabbage, and avocado onto nori sheets and roll tightly with a sushi-mat. Wet the edge of each sheet to seal shut. Cut into 1-inch thick pieces with a wet knife. Dip pieces into Miso Dip (see below). My favorite raw recipe!

<u>Miso Dip for Nori Rolls:</u>
1 tsp. Unpasteurized Miso
1 Cup Distilled Water

Mix miso with distilled water until soup-like, smooth, and watery.

Captain's Powerhouse

1 Young Coconut (Juice and Pulp)
1 Large Avocado
2 Handfuls Wild or Organic Greens

Drain coconut juice into a Vita-Mix. Crack coconut in half, scoop out jelly-like pulp into Vita-Mix. Discard coconut husk. Discard pit and skin of avocado and put avocado pulp into Vita-Mix. Add two handfuls of greens. Blend to desired consistency. Drink 30 minutes after work-out for best results.

Avo Soup

2 Large Avocados
1 Medium Cucumber
1 Medium Tomato
1/2 Cup Loose Corn
1 Cup Chopped Zucchini
1/4 Cup Chopped Green Onion
Dash of Cilantro
Distilled Water

Discard avocado pits and skins. Put 1-1/2 avocado fruits, cucumber, tomato, and cilantro into blender. Blend, adding distilled water for desired consistency. Pour into a bowl. Chop 1/2 avocado into small cubes. Put avocado, zucchini, corn, and onions on top of soup. Delicious! People eat *cooked* soup?

Datenut Shake

1 Cup Soaked Almonds
4 Medjool or 6 Barhi Dates
Distilled Water

Remove and discard date pits. Blend soaked almonds and date fruits with distilled water to desired consistency.

Go-Through-A-Brick-Wall Juice

6 Ounces Sprouted Wheatberries
6 Handfuls of Wild or Organic Dandelion Greens
1 Ounce Ginger Root

Put 3-day sprouted wheatberries through juicer. Put ginger through juicer. Put greens through juicer. Pour juice into large glass. For information on how to sprout wheat, read "The Wheatgrass Book" by Ann Wigmore. This drink is electrical -- quite a jolt!

CW Trail Mix

4 Ounces Macadamias
4 Ounces Almonds
4 Ounces Pistachios
4 Ounces Raisins (with seeds)

Mix all together in a bag (powerful combo!).

Fruit Smoothie

2 Large Manzano Bananas
3 Ounces Soaked Sunflower Seeds
2 Cups Berries
Distilled Water

Peel bananas and discard peels. Put bananas into a Vita-Mix blender. Add sunflower seeds into blender. Add berries into blender. Pour in distilled water and blend to desired consistency.

Raw Burritos

4 Large Avocados
1 Medium Red Onion
3 Red Jalapeno Peppers
1 Head Red Cabbage
2 Yellow Limes

Discard pits and skins of avocados. Put avocado fruits into a large bowl. Discard seeds of jalapeno peppers. Dice peppers and put into bowl. Dice onion and put into bowl. Mix ingredients (this is your filler). Spoon out filler into unbroken red cabbage leaves, squeeze lime juice onto filler, and wrap each leaf around filler to create "raw burritos."

The Protein Myth

5 Ounces Wheatgrass Juice
1 Young Coconut (Juice Only)

Put wheatgrass through Miracle Wheatgrass Juicer until you have 5 ounces of juice. Pour into large glass. Add juice from young coconut. For information on how to grow your own wheatgrass, read "The Wheatgrass Book" by Ann Wigmore.

Fire Water

1 Orange or Red Habanero Pepper
1 Medium Orange
4 Cups Distilled Water

Put habanero pepper in juicer. Peel orange and discard orange peel. Put orange fruit through juicer. Pour 4 cups of distilled water into juicer to flush out remaining nutrients. Pour Fire Water into pitcher and serve. It is best to drink this 30 minutes before a meal.

Pre-Work-Out Drink

3 Stalks Celery
2 Medium Apples

Put foods through juicer. Drink 1 hour before work-out. Excellent sodium/potassium balance.

Ants In A Canoe

2 Large Apples
2 Cups Soaked Almonds
2 Ounces Raisins (with seeds)

Soak almonds in distilled water for 12 hours. Put soaked almonds through a Champion or Green Power Juicer, using the blank plate. This will make almond butter. Cut apples into quarters. Remove and discard seeds. Spread almond butter on apples, cover with raisins. Great snack. Kelly Alexander taught me this one.

Fats Avocado Salad

3-4 Handfuls Wild or Organic Greens
2 Large Avocados
30-40 Olives
4 tsp. Extra-Virgin Cold-Pressed Olive Oil
1 Medium Orange

Discard pits of olives, pits and skins of avocados, and orange peel. Make a bed of wild or organic greens and/or herbs, add avocado fruit, olives, olive oil, and add juice of the orange to taste. Greens and fats are your body-builders. Powerful salad!

Green Juice

3 Handfuls Kale
1 Cucumber
3 Handfuls Spinach
3 Stalks Celery
2 Handfuls Parsley

Put all foods into Champion or G. P. juicer.

Applenut Salad

1 Head Red Leaf Lettuce
1 Cup Sunflower Sprouts
1 Diced Apple
1/2 Cup Chopped Walnuts
1 Cup Grapes

Make a bed of lettuce and sprouts. Put apple, walnuts, and grapes on top of bed.

Blue Cream

2 Manzano Bananas
2 Cherimoyas
1 Cup Blueberries

Peel bananas and discard peels. Peel cherimoyas and discard peels and seeds. Put bananas, cherimoyas, and blueberries into Vita-Mix blender.

Appendix D:

Seasonal Produce Availability

Eating seasonal fruits and vegetables is Nature's way of telling you what to eat and when. Eating foods when they are in season is an integral part of health and the importance of doing so cannot be overemphasized. Thus, I have included the following information regarding seasonal produce availability. Though varieties of each food may differ, this compilation lists each food's peak season(s) according to a survey of Farmer's Markets conducted within the United States in 1998.

Compiled by Jolie Thedell & Stephen Arlin

Food	Season
Acorn Squash	Summer
Almond	Fall
Ambrosia Melon	Summer
Anise	Fall
Apple	Fall, Early Winter
Apricot	Summer
Arrame	All seasons
Artichoke	Fall
Arugula	Winter

Food	**Season**
Asian Pear	Fall, Early Winter
Asparagus	Spring
Atemoya	Late Winter, Spring
Avocado	All seasons
Banana	All seasons
Basil	All seasons
Beet	Fall, Winter, Spring
Blackberry	Early Summer
Black Sapote	Summer
Blood Orange	Winter
Blueberry	Summer
Bok Choy	Winter
Boysenberry	Early Summer
Brazil Nut	Fall
Breadfruit	Early Summer
Broccoli	Winter
Brussels Sprouts	Fall
Cabbage	Winter
Canistel	Spring
Cantaloupe	Summer
Carambola	Spring
Carob	Spring
Carrot	All seasons
Casaba Melon	Summer
Cashew Apple	Fall
Cassia	Spring
Cauliflower	Winter
Celery	Fall

Food	Season
Chard	Fall, Winter, Spring
Chayote	Fall
Cherimoya	Late Winter, Spring
Cherry	Spring
Chestnut	Fall
Chicory	Fall, Winter, Spring
Chive	All seasons
Cilantro	All seasons
Cranberry	Fall
Crenshaw Melon	Summer
Coconut	All seasons
Collard	Fall, Winter, Spring
Corn	Summer
Currant	Spring
Cucumber	Summer
Dandelion	Late Winter, Spring
Date	Fall, Winter
Dill	All seasons
Dulse	All seasons
Durian	Spring, Summer
Eggplant	Summer
Endive	Fall
Escarole	Fall, Winter, Spring
Fennel	Winter
Feijoa	Fall
Fiddlehead Fern	Fall, Winter, Spring
Fig	Late Summer
Frisee	Fall, Winter, Spring

Food	**Season**
Garlic	All seasons
Ginger	All seasons
Ginseng	All seasons
Gooseberry	Summer
Gourd	Fall
Grapefruit	Winter, Early Spring
Grape	Summer
Green Bean	Early Summer
Green Butter	Fall, Winter, Spring
Green Leaf	Fall, Winter, Spring
Green Oak	Fall, Winter, Spring
Guava	Spring
Hazelnut	Fall
Hijiki	All seasons
Honeydew Melon	Summer
Huckleberry	Late Summer
Jakfruit	Spring
Jicama	All seasons
Jujube	Fall
Kale	Fall, Winter, Spring
Kiwi	Winter, Early Spring
Kohlrabi	Fall, Winter, Spring
Kombu	All seasons
Kumquat	Winter
Lamb's Quarters	Winter
Leeks	Fall
Lemonberry	Summer
Lemongrass	Winter

Food	Season
Food	**Season**
Lemon	Winter, Early Spring
Lime	Winter, Early Spring
Loganberry	Early Summer
Longan	Summer
Loquat	Early Summer
Lotus	All seasons
Lovage	Spring, Summer
Lychee	Summer
Macadamia Nut	Fall
Mache	Fall, Winter, Spring
Malva	Late Fall, Winter
Mamey Sapote	Spring
Mango	Late Spring, Summer
Mangosteen	Fall, Early Summer
Marjoram	All seasons
Mint	All seasons
Mizuna	Fall, Winter, Spring
Monstera Deliciosia	Late Spring, Summer
Mountain Apple	Spring
Mulberry	Summer
Mustard	Fall, Winter, Spring
Nasturtium	Summer
Nectarine	Summer
Nori	All seasons
Okra	Fall
Olive	Fall, Winter, Spring
Onion	All seasons
Orange	Winter, Early Spring

Food	**Season**
Oregano	All seasons
Papaya	All seasons
Parsley	All seasons
Parsnip	Late Fall
Passionfruit	Fall
Peach	Summer
Peanut	All seasons
Pear	Fall, Early Winter
Pea	Spring
Pecan	Fall
Pepper	Late Summer, Fall
Peppergrass	All seasons
Persimmon	Fall
Pineapple	All seasons
Pine Nut	Fall
Pistachio	Fall
Plantain	All seasons
Plum	Early Summer
Pomegranate	Fall
Pomelo	Winter
Potato	All seasons
Prickly Pear	Fall
Pumpkin	Fall
Purslane	All seasons
Quince	Fall, Early Winter
Radicchio	Fall, Winter, Spring
Radish	Fall, Winter
Rambutan	Summer

Food	**Season**
Raspberry	Early Summer
Red Butter	Fall, Winter, Spring
Red Chard	Fall, Winter, Spring
Red Oak	Fall, Winter, Spring
Red Orach	Fall, Winter, Spring
Rhubarb	Spring
Rosemary	All seasons
Rutabaga	Late Fall
Sage	All seasons
Sapodilla	Spring
Savory	Fall, Winter, Spring
Scallion	All seasons
Sea Palm	All seasons
Shallot	All seasons
Sharlyn Melon	Summer
Snow Pea	Early Spring
Sorrel	Late Winter
Sourgrass	All seasons
Soursop	Late Winter, Spring
Spinach	Winter
Strawberry	Summer
Sugar Apple	Late Winter, Spring
Summer Squash	Summer
Sunflower	Summer
Surinam Cherry	Spring
Sweet Potato	Fall
Tamarind	Spring
Tangelo	Winter, Early Spring

Food	**Season**
Tangerine	Winter, Early Spring
Tango	Fall, Winter, Spring
Tarragon	All seasons
Tat Soi	Fall, Winter, Spring
Thyme	All seasons
Tiger Lily	Summer
Tomatillo	Late Summer
Tomato	Summer
Travissio	Fall, Winter, Spring
Turnip	Winter
Ugli Fruit	Winter, Early Spring
Velvet Apple	Late Summer
Violet	Summer
Wakame	All seasons
Walnut	Fall
Watercress	Fall, Winter, Spring
Watermelon	Summer
Wheatgrass	All seasons
White Sapote	Winter, Summer
Wintercress	All seasons
Winter Squash	Fall, Winter
Yam	Fall
Zucchini	Early Summer

There are many thousands more edible foods in the world. You could eat a different raw plant food every day of your life and *still* not try them all! Does anyone still think that eating a raw-food diet is boring?

Appendix E:

Photographs

Preacher Curls: Position yourself with your chest against the bench, your arms extending over it. Take hold of an E-Z bar with an underhand grip. Curl the bar all the way up and then lower it again to full extension, resisting the weight on the way down. Flex the biceps at the top of the movement.

Lat Machine Pulldowns - Close Grip: Grasp the handles with a close grip with your knees hooked under the support. Pull the grip down smoothly until your hands slightly touch the top of your chest. Release, extend the arms again, and feel the lats fully stretch.

Lat Machine Pulldowns - Wide Grip: Using a long bar, grasp it with a wide, overhand grip with your knees hooked under the support. Pull the bar down smoothly until it touches the back of your neck, making the upper back do the work. Release, extend the arms again, and feel the lats fully stretch.

Dumbbell Flys: Lie on a bench holding dumbbells at arm's length above you, palms facing one another. Lower the weights out and down to either side in a wide arc as far as you can, feeling the pectoral muscles stretch to their maximum. The palms should remain facing each other throughout the movement. Bring the weights to a complete stop at a lower point than the bench, then lift them back up to the starting position along the same wide arc.

Dumbbell Pullovers: Lie across a bench with your feet flat on the floor. Place a dumbbell on the floor behind your head. Reach back and grasp the weight. Keeping your arms bent, raise the weight and bring it just over your head to your chest. Lower the weight slowly back to the starting position without touching the floor, feeling the lats stretch out to their fullest.

Triceps Cable Pushdowns: Hook a bar to an overhead cable and pulley, stand close to the bar and grasp it with an overhand grip, hands about 10 inches apart. Keep your elbows tucked in close to your body and stationary. Press the bar down as far as possible, locking out your arms and feeling the triceps contract fully. Release and let the bar come up as far as possible without moving the elbows.

Standing Curls: Stand with feet a few inches apart and grasp an E-Z bar with an underhanded grip, hands about shoulder width apart. Let the bar hang down at arm's length in front of you. Curl the bar out and up in a wide arc and bring it up as high as you can, your elbows close to the body and stationary. Lower the weight, following the same arc and resisting the weight all the way down until your arms are fully extended.

Bent-Over Barbell Rows: Standing with your feet a few inches apart, grasp the bar with a wide, overhand grip. With your knees slightly bent, bend forward until your upper body is about parallel to the floor. Keep your back straight and let the bar hang at arm's length below you, almost touching the shinbone. Lift the bar upward until it touches the upper abdominals, then slowly lower it again to the starting position.

Swimming is an excellent form of aerobic exercise. I recommend doing laps under water whilst holding your breath. Also, treading water for 30 minutes after an intense work-out really gives your body an extra boost and gives you an edge over everyone else!

Since adopting The Raw-Food Diet several years ago, I have experienced a major increase in my body's resistance to extreme weather temperatures. I am much more resistant to cold and hot weather now than I was before. Snow-skiing without a shirt (or clothes) feels great!

Recommended Reading

Blatant Raw-Foodist Propaganda, Joe Alexander
Diet For A New America, John Robbins
Edible Wild Plants, Elias & Dykeman
Enzyme Nutrition, Dr. Edward Howell
Fruitarian Diet And Physical Rejuvenation,
  Dr. O.L.M. Abramowski
**How To Win An Argument With A Cooked-Food
  Eater**, Stephen Arlin
IS Philosophy, Stephen Arlin
Man's Higher Consciousness, Hilton Hotema
Mucusless Diet Healing System, Arnold Ehret
Nature's First Law: The Raw-Food Diet, Arlin,
  Dini, & Wolfe
On Form And Actuality, David Wolfe
Perfect Body, Roe Gallo
Primal Mothering In A Modern World, Hygeia
  Halfmoon
Raw Courage World, R.C. Dini
Raw Fruit & Vegetable Recipes, Phyllis Avery
The Raw Truth: The Art Of Loving Foods,
  Jeremy Safron & Renee Underkoffler
The Sunfood Diet Success System, David Wolfe
The Wheatgrass Book, Ann Wigmore

All books available through:
Nature's First Law 1-800-205-2350

Organizations

Nature's First Law
PO Box 900202
San Diego, CA 92190 USA
619-645-7282
800-205-2350 - orders
Internet: http://www.rawfood.com
E-mail: nature@io-online.com
Nature's First Law is The World's Premier Source
of Raw-Food Diet Books, Juicers,
Videos, and Audio Tapes.

The Date People
P.O. Box 808
Niland, CA 92257
760-359-3211
The world's best dates.

The FRESH Network
17 Higher Green
South Brent, Devon
TQ10 9PL England
+44-1364-73993
E-mail: fresh@eclipse.co.uk
Fruitarian & Raw Energy Support & Help
Director: Susie Miller

Fruitarian Network News
(4 issues/year)
Support for Fruitarians world-wide.
Director: Rene Beresford * Regular Features:
International Contacts * Fruit Poetry * Self-Help
Information * Interviews * Fruit Facts.
$41/year. To subscribe write, call, or e-mail:
Nature's First Law
PO Box 900202, San Diego, CA 92190 USA
800-205-2350 -- E-mail: nature@io-online.com

Just Eat An Apple Magazine
(6 issues/year)
From the Nature's First Law head office.
An uncompromising approach to the RAW
lifestyle! * Regular Features: Interviews * Food &
Sex * Fascinating Raw Philosophy * What's Raw,
What's Cooked * Networking Contacts *
What's Happening in The Raw-Food World.
$30/year ($40/year foreign). 20 pages/issue.
To subscribe write, call, or e-mail:
Nature's First Law
PO Box 900202, San Diego, CA 92190 USA
800-205-2350 -- E-mail: nature@io-online.com

Karyn's Fresh Corner
3351 N. Lincoln
Chicago, IL 60657
773-296-6990
Raw-food restaurant in Chicago, Illinois.

Living Nutrition Magazine
(4 issues/year)

The World's premier magazine dedicated to helping health seekers learn how to succeed with eating our natural diet of raw foods! Excellent format, high quality, 32+ pages. Regular Features: Dietary Transition Help * Physical Fitness Pointers * Healthful Eating Guidelines * Networking Contacts Raw-Food Events * Raw-Food Recipes * Literature Reviews * Natural Healing Education * Testimonials * Biodynamic Organiculture Articles * Raw-Food Parenting * Nature's First Law Column.

$20/1-year subscription (US$25 foreign),
$30/2-year subscription (US$40 foreign)

To subscribe write, call, or e-mail:

Nature's First Law

PO Box 900202, San Diego, CA 92190 USA

800-205-2350 -- E-mail: nature@io-online.com

Naturliche Gesundheit
Helmut Wandmaker

Muhlenberg 15

D-25782 Tellingstedt

Germany

Helmut Wandmaker is the foremost promoter of The Raw-Food Diet in Germany.

Planet Health
319 E. 9th Street
New York, NY 10003
800-398-6237
E-mail: helthbound@aol.com
Ed Lieb & Matthew Grace
Raw-Food Diet promoters in New York City.
Produce a television program
"Accent On Wellness."
Major distributor of Rebounders.

Raw Experience Restaurant
42 Baldwin Ave.
Paia, HI 96779 USA
808-579-9729
Raw-food restaurant in Maui, Hawaii.

Raw Experience Restaurant
1224 9th Ave.
San Francisco, CA 94122 USA
415-665-6519
Raw-food restaurant
in San Francisco, California.

The Raw Truth Restaurant
Las Vegas, NV USA
702-454-6060
Raw-food restaurant
in Las Vegas, Nevada.

Additional Copies of Raw Power!

Additional copies of **Raw Power!** may be ordered directly from Nature's First Law. One book is $11.95 plus $3.00 shipping and handling ($9.00 s&h if outside the United States or Canada). For each additional book please add $1.00 shipping (add $6.00 s&h if outside the United States or Canada). California residents add 7.75% sales tax. **Bulk discounts are available.**

If you have any questions or comments about any of the material contained in this book, feel free to write, call, or e-mail Stephen Arlin and/or Nature's First Law. We seek correspondence with all like-minded individuals seeking the glorious path to Paradise on Earth.

Also, check out the **Nature's First Law Catalog**. Each Catalog contains the highest-quality books, juicers, booklets, video tapes, and audio tapes on The Raw-Food Diet, Fruitarianism, and related material. To receive a free copy of the Nature's First Law Catalog please write, call, or e-mail Nature's First Law.

Nature's First Law
PO Box 900202
San Diego, CA 92190 U.S.A.
(619) 645-7282
(800) 205-2350 - orders only

E-mail: nature@io-online.com
Internet Homepage: http://www.rawfood.com